# THE ENCHANTER

LILA AZAM ZANGANEH

# THE
# ENCHANTER

*Nabokov and Happiness*

W. W. NORTON & COMPANY / NEW YORK • LONDON

For information about special discounts for bulk purchases, please contact
W. W. Norton Special Sales at specialsales@wwnorton.com or 800-233-4830

Manufacturing by Courier Westford
Book design by Ellen Cipriano
Production manager: Julia Druskin

Library of Congress Cataloging-in-Publication Data

Azam Zanganeh, Lila.
    The enchanter : Nabokov and happiness / Lila Azam Zanganeh. — 1st ed.
        p. cm.
    Includes bibliographical references and index.
    ISBN 978-0-393-07992-0 (hardcover)
    1. Nabokov, Vladimir Vladimirovich, 1899–1977—Criticism and interpretation.
    2. Happiness in literature. I. Title.
        PG3476.N3Z575 2011
        813'.54—dc22

                                                                                2011004729

W. W. Norton & Company, Inc.
500 Fifth Avenue, New York, N.Y. 10110
www.wwnorton.com

W. W. Norton & Company Ltd.
Castle House, 75/76 Wells Street, London W1T 3QT

1  2  3  4  5  6  7  8  9  0

*To the three women who started my story——*

*Zahra Nosratian, my grandmother, who was ever searching*
*Nilou Ghodsi Azam Zanganeh, my mother, who wove the dream*
*Nicole Aragi, who lent me her colors*

I trust the ravishing promises of the still breathing, still revolving verse, my face is wet with tears, my heart is bursting with happiness, and I know that this happiness is the greatest thing existing on earth.

VLADIMIR NABOKOV, "TORPID SMOKE"

A BURST

A PART OF IT

A
BRIGHT DOT
OF MEMORY

A DRE

THROUGH
THE LOOKING GLASS

sub rosa
fata morgana
gloamin
umbelifer cochlea
heavenlogged scimitar

THE CRUNCH

PARTICLES

HAPPINESS

COUNTERCLOCKWISE

A PRACTICAL HANDBOOK

TRANSPARENT ABYSS

SIX MAD HATTERS

MER'S EXTRAVAGANT

A
READER'S ADVENTURE

SUNDRY
DETAILS

HAPPINESS

NATURAL
&
UNNATURAL

APRIL ARIZONA

MAY FOLLOW THE ITINERARY
OR CHOOSE YOUR OWN.

# CONTENTS

# WHY READ THIS OR ANY OTHER BOOKS?

I have always dreaded reading and books. Yet I am about to tell the story of a handful of books which turned my fortunes. The adventures on which they sent me were entirely imaginary. Or at least, at first they were. They required no visits to reclusive Amazonian tribes or inhabitants of remote Muscovy. They took no toll on lazy feet and reluctant stomachs.

For there I was, on a late afternoon in a North American city of the eastern seaboard, lounging on a plump couch under a bell-shaped lamp. The spring, outside, was still young. It was cloudy and cold. And night would soon creep into the living room. I was about to pore over a chosen text, when—well, that's when the first difficulties arose.

The irresistible desire to fall asleep. It's a devious impulse to fight, so my personal preference is to give in, and rather sooner than later.

After a brief spell of light slumber, eyes wide open, I collected myself. Soon, I was stretching languorously, getting up, sampling a tangerine, circling round the room on several random quests, pretending to ponder the beauty of an opening line, before grudgingly making my way back to the couch. This time, I figured I might be better off sitting upright. Then it happened. The dread. The compressed letters of the alphabet dealt in terrifying order. On checking a few hours earlier, the verdict had been unequivocal: 589 pages. The horror. I ran in my mind a line by Hobbes whom, as a matter of general principle, I am not used to quoting to myself. "If I had read as much as other men, I should be as ignorant." Hobbes reassured me, alas, very briefly.

For now, with *Ada* at an oblique angle, I plowed through the strange sentences of page 1. After the letters somehow coalesced into words and began making a semblance of sense, the second hurdle was the abhorrent topography of the paragraph. "Dolly, an only child, born in Bras, married in 1840, at the tender and wayward age of fifteen, General Ivan Durmanov, Commander of Yukon Fortress and peaceful country gentleman, with lands in the Severn Tories (Severnïya Territorii), that tessellated protectorate still lovingly called 'Russian' Estoty, which commingles, granoblastically and organically, with 'Russian' Canady, otherwise 'French' Estoty, where not only French, but Macedonian and Bavarian settlers enjoy a halcyon climate under our Stars and Stripes." Good heavens! That gruesome maze! I snapped the book shut. Moments later, with a pang of intellectual guilt, I opened it again.

Here and there, sundry things started beckoning on the next pages . . . A Butterfly Orchis in a forest of ancestral pines, sun flecks and bruised wings gliding at high noon over a summer day, a glistening morning of green rain. I read on, striving to see, dwelling on the shades if not the turns of the unfolding story, which at present mostly amounted to a bizarre vortex. But I kept my cool and proceeded. Literary rumor has it that one must reach the magical *one hundredth* page to inhabit the universe of a novel. So I pushed my way into the pages, scrupulously resting my eyes on every word, even as anxiety loomed at the idea of having to absorb nearly everything (a resilient obsession). Hence I must confirm in passing what, surely, you already suspect—I have never been, indeed cannot be, a voracious reader. I am seized by such a sense of panic at sentence after sentence that I often find myself reading every line several times before moving along, or turning a page.

Granted, reading this closely is, by most mental-health prescriptions, a uselessly painstaking task. Why even bother? Emerson—a voracious reader if ever there was one—would likely deem such a fastidious reader a damn fool. "We are too civil to books," he once told a student. "For a few golden sentences we will turn over and actually read a volume of 4 or 5 hundred pages." Why not be blatantly uncivil to this one writer, Vladimir Nabokov, author of *Lolita*, *Speak, Memory*, and *Ada, or Ardor*? And while I am at it, why read these or any other books? Why confront oneself with the generalized terror of countless unread pages, the squadrons of words that will eventually defeat us, if only because we read against the clock?

The answer, in my eyes, has always beamed with clarity. We read to reenchant the world. There is, of course, a cost, even for the more limber reader. Deciphering, trudging into unknown regions, making one's way through an intricate atlas of sentences, startling darkness, unfamiliar flora and fauna. Yet should one carry on with stubborn curiosity, a conquering spirit, now and then a sumptuous vista will emerge, a sun-shot landscape, gleaming sea-creatures.

To begin this journey, we may first *divine* which books we truly desire or need. In my case, call it intuition, or fate (a family affair to be chronicled later). But I had expected to find enchanters and demons in Nabokov. Shuddering magic. The stuff of fairy-tales, "noble iridescent creatures with translucent talons and mightily beating wings." The rest, in truth, was something akin to falling in love, a haunting feeling of native otherness.

It has to do with the wiles of a new language. A language whose twists and turns seem all but reinvented. One perceives a radiant arc, revels for a suspended moment in its light, its poise. It is like penetrating an elemental mystery, an invisible structure, rendered visible at once through an inflection of words, a rippling of sounds, resonating with the exact tone of even the most trivial or vilest thing. A whisper following you everywhere, summarizing existence.

To seize upon this is our chance to become what Nabokov calls a "creative reader," which is to say, a fellow dreamer, observing the minute detail of the world. As such, we are "crashing to our death from the top story of our birth and wondering with an immortal Alice in Wonderland at the patterns of the passing wall," VN writes. "These asides of the spirit, these footnotes in the volume of life are the highest form of consciousness." The novelist is an immortal Alice in the real world. His inspiration, a stab of rapture and recapture, perceiving past, present, and future in a single instant, conjuring the cycle of pure time, and thus quietly blowing clocks apart. As readers, we might touch upon this miracle. It is something that defies bleak common sense, and smiles secretly in the face of the grinding logic of linear time. A childlike capacity to wonder at trifles, to overlook gravity and feast on "the irrational, the illogical, the inexplicable" pigments of beauty.

To do so, we may first try to imagine a novel with maddening precision and fully explore that marvelous optical toy opening views of images within images. Because each image lost is a lost occasion for happiness. And as we flip through the pages, we may also look for a nether side—that is, a secluded world we are each in our own way prompted to dream, a world that both is and no longer is the novel in hand, since it pertains solely to us. Then, and only then, will the colors and schemes of our new surroundings meld with a reality that will lose "the quotes it wore like claws." The human adventure will be complete, by a feat of imagination.

That is where I discovered the very texture of happiness. Literature—and Nabokov in particular—became not a manual, but an experience in happiness. VN, in his linguistic genius and trilingual grace, awakened it more vividly than anyone else I had ever read.

Of course, it might appear unsettling at first to celebrate happiness according to Vladimir Nabokov, a writer so often associated with moral and sexual malaise. Yet I am convinced that he is the great writer of happiness. And by happiness, I do not mean a general sense of besotted wellbeing and satisfaction (for are not only cows content in that sense?). VN's happiness is a singular way of seeing, marveling, and grasping, in other words, of netting the light particles tingling around us. It belongs to his own definition of art as curiosity and ecstasy, an art which spurs

us in the exhilarating task of consciousness. Even in darkness or demise, Nabokov tells us, things quiver with lam-
bent beauty. Light is to be found everywhere. Though the
heart of the matter is not to gape beatifically. The heart
of the matter is to recapture light through the prism of
language and knowledge of the most exquisite kind. This
knowledge, to the nth degree, contains "perfect felicity."
For with it, we turn what might seem like matter-of-fact,
everyday occurrences into unique surprises, crafted with
infinite cunning and outstanding intelligence. And luckily,
in the Nabokovian landscape, the microscope's limpid well
is hidden in plain view, tempting us to peer through it at
every second.

Perhaps I should add that being the great writer of happiness does not signify telling happy stories with platitudinous
happy characters. The deep joyousness I found in *Lolita* or *Ada*
takes its source elsewhere. It is connected to an experience
of the edge, an experience of limits (in its quasi-mathematical
sense of an open-end), which in turn becomes one of extreme
poetry. And this poetry is bliss, or as VN called it in his native
Russian, "*blazhenstvo*." Though as always with Nabokov, bliss
is not a generic form of ecstasy. Within his pages, ecstasy is
concealed in fiercely original tales of desire driven to a near-
folly, no matter the consequences. So that paradoxically, bliss
is not bereft of egotism and cruelty. Sometimes this bliss is
even "beyond happiness," a realm of unearthly inebriation.
There, phrases appear to belong to a new plane of sensitiv-

ity. A language recombining elements with such astonishing artistry and ardor as to obliterate the very limits of language as we knew it.

When I initially contemplated writing this book, I thought I would essentially write *about* happiness. As a reader, I felt I would diligently apply myself to researching, thinking, and composing. But then, as the writing began, a tenuous detail of the Nabokovian universe would suddenly call, as though by a magnetic pull, to a fragment of my own life, real or maybe imagined. Things I had never seemed to have articulated before, or had barely noticed, came rushing to the surface.

I strove to pin down the right words and play with them until their melody matched my mental image as accurately as possible. And while I did this, something shifted in my narrator's "eye." The real-life "I," the one writing here and now, slowly dissolved into a more imaginary "I," seeing and reinventing through a Nabokovian lens. Unity of font, form, and narrative lines gave way to a new logic which followed sinuous paths. The true story of an ecstatic writer blended with the looking-glass fancy of a maniacal reader. Flashes of VN's memories summoned fresh colors; fragments of stories evoked untold stories; sentences caused fitful echoes. Time and again, I remembered a short story VN had published in Berlin, in which a young Russian poet, though aware of writing simple, youthful poems, experiences absolute happiness even in the faintest blushes of creation.

*The Enchanter* is the record of an adventure. Every chapter—as seen on the opening map—is one idea of happiness. And the book unfolds through fifteen Alice-like variations, rambles where, at times, beginning and end are but one and the same, and inroads turn out to be bright mirrors.

# THE ENCHANTER

*"I, Vladimir Nabokov, salute you, life!"*

# PROLOGUE

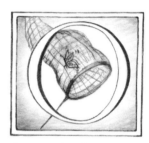ne cobalt-blue morning of butterfly hunting, in August 1971, after climbing a Swiss mountain, looking tanned and serene, net in hand, Vladimir Nabokov told his son Dmitri he had fulfilled all he ever dreamed and was a supremely happy man. It is on this mountainous peak that I like to imagine him, VN, exclaiming like his elated creature Van Veen: "I, Vladimir Nabokov, salute you, life!"

Dmitri snapped a photo that day as his seventy-two-year-old father stood on the summit of La Videmanette, at 7,000 feet above sea level, peering out, his back slightly arched, white cap, light beige coat, dark bermudas and hiking boots, thick white socks rolled around the ankles. In his hands lay the little Band-Aid box he'd been using for decades to store his butterflies. With the alpine meadows

and patches of pine trees behind him, he stood contemplat-
ing the horizon, observing, perhaps, the miniature details
of the nearby town of Rougemont, as the sun formed speckles on his forehead and the left side of his nose.

To this moment, I see him there, resting with striking
poise under his own clear and quirky firmament. Like his
Russian pen name, "Sirin," an elusive bird of paradise.

## CHAPTER I

# A DREAMER'S EXTRAVAGANT HAPPINESS

(Where the writer dies into an unfinished book
and the reader embarks on a posthumous search
to track him down)

For the moon never beams, without bringing me dreams . . .

abokov died on July 2nd, 1977. I
was ten months old. Roughly four
hundred miles had separated us. In
sum, we had got off to an unfortunate start. He would remain forever
unaware of my puny existence.

Merely four months before I was born, Nabokov felt his
death was near. He had just turned seventy-seven. On April
24, 1976, to be precise, this is what he wrote in his diary: "At
1 A.M. was raised from brief sleep by horrible anguish of the
'this-is-it' sort. *Discreetly* screamed, hoping to wake Véra in
next room yet failing to succeed (because I felt quite alright)."

He had always been a wretched sleeper, but years were
taking their toll, and the most potent pills could no longer
sedate his private ghosts. He would lie awake much of the
night, tormented by his imagination spinning away in the
dark. As the pills grew stronger, VN even suffered eerie

hallucinations and had to toss the devious tablets at once. But worst of all, every evening, was the creeping trepidation of the ticking hours ahead.

The previous summer, a late morning of July 1975, for the very first time, while butterfly hunting on an alpine slope, Nabokov had fallen and slid a steep 150 feet, losing his net to the branch of a neighboring fir. Inching warily toward it, he had slid yet again and had been unable to get back on his feet. The situation caused—as absurd situations often did with Nabokov—an irrepressible fit of laughter, so intense that the people in the cable car rolling above presumed he was lying at his leisure, frolicking in the afternoon sun. It was only when the cable-car conductor caught sight of VN a second time that he suspected something was amiss and ordered a stretcher to be sent out, two and a half hours after his fall. Though Nabokov was not severely injured, his net would forever clasp its branch "like Ovid's lyre," as he later jotted down. An invisible fracture had furtively opened. VN, who had battled against the prison of time as far back as memory would take him, was now feeling time's onslaught. A "horrible shock," he noted.

That autumn, a tumor in his prostate called for general anesthesia, which, to the writer of heightened consciousness, was nothing short of an experiment in a mortal's ridicule—the humiliation of etherizing the senses like a miniature rehearsal of death. Besides, his insomnia had become chronic, and he was unusually agitated. Unable to stand the limbo of convalescence, and despite persistent warnings from his doctors, he also picked up his novel in progress, *The Original of Laura: Dying Is Fun*, on the white 3-by-5-inch index cards he'd been using for decades. About a year before, Nabokov had felt its first little throb: "Inspiration. Radiant insomnia. The flavour and snows of beloved alpine slopes. A novel *without* an I, without a he, but with the narrator, the *gliding eye*, being implied throughout."

By April 1976, at the Montreux Palace Hotel, Véra and Vladimir merrily toasted to VN's seventy-seventh birthday, and Nabokov scribbled as many as five or six index cards every afternoon. From then on, however, he would tackle countless setbacks. Later that year, he fell on his head and walked with visible strain thereafter, suffering horrific backaches and occasional temperatures. A mysterious infection seemed to plague him and repeatedly sent him to various Swiss clinics and hospitals. There, to wile away time, he read much of the day: a new guide titled *Butterflies of North America*, and a remarkably literal translation of Dante's *Inferno*. But mostly, in high VN fashion, he read to himself the novel that was lucid as colored glass in his mind—the yet unfinished *Original of Laura*. Nearly every morning, in a state of quasi-trance, he read and perfected *Laura*. Just as all his other novels before they were actually written, he pictured this last one in his mind like a film reel about to be developed on his immaculate index cards. Alone in his hospital room, he even recited it, as later recorded, to "a small dream audience in a walled garden. My audience consisted of peacocks, pigeons, my long-dead parents, two cypresses, several young nurses crouching around, and a family doctor so old as to be almost invisible."

In late July, Nabokov was reclaiming ground on life. But he knew that in nearly twenty years, this was the only summer to elapse without butterfly hunts. By the end of September, back in his hotel suite, he was tremendously weakened. He confessed to his wife that he didn't much take to hospitals, "Only because you're not there. I would never mind a hospital stay if I could take you, wrap you up in my top pocket and take you with me." Yet even with Véra by his side, after so many months of illness, a dreadful languor had taken hold of him. *The Original of Laura* all but composed in his imagination, VN was, to his own dismay, too exhausted to write it. And when the ever-nosy reporter inquired about his culinary diet, Nabokov quipped, "My literary regime is more fancy, but two hours of meditation, between 2 A.M. and 4 A.M. when the effect of a first sleeping pill evaporates and that of a second one has not begun, and a spell of writing in the afternoon, are about all my new novel needs." As late as February 1977, he announced that when the winds turned he would take a journey to his cherished American West. By the spring of 1977, he still avidly dreamed of a trip to Israel where, he fancied, he would be exploring Middle Eastern butterflies at long last (a decade earlier, he'd said, "I also intend to collect butterflies in Peru or in Iran before I pupate.") But his gait, so vigorous two summers past, was now that of an elderly man, and he was overwhelmed with the onerous literary tasks he had set himself: editing the imperfect translations of previous novels, and lending earthly shape to *Laura*. Friends were perplexed at the sight of a waning VN. Véra kept, in everyone's eyes, as composed a façade as ever.

Presently, Nabokov's spirits appeared to lift, though in March 1977 his diary ominously records another relapse: "Everything begins anew." Two months later, back at his desk, he still toiled away at *Laura*, still played the occasional hoax on favorite visitors. But by May 18, his handwriting drifting to a scrawl, he noted: "Mild delirium, temp. 37.5°. Is it possible that everything starts anew?" It was proving nearly impossible to focus, and on one fateful night, VN the "lexicomaniac" lost at Russian Scrabble to his sister Elena for the first time in his life. In a matter of weeks, high fevers struck with full force and Nabokov was transferred to a hospital in Lausanne. There, Véra sternly told a befuddled doctor, who confidently announced Nabokov was recovering, that as far as she was concerned he was dying.

In those last days, Dmitri recalls his father whispering to him how proud he was that his son was about to leave for his Munich opera début. He recalls those hours spent in Munich as more blissful than any he would know in the years to come, simply because "Father still existed." Yet on his return, he noticed a dusk of resignation in his father's gaze. "Now and then," Dmitri later wrote, "one had an inkling of how deeply hurt he felt at the thought of being suddenly cut off from a life whose every detail gave him joy, and from a creative process in its fullest swing."

Véra said in passing that she did not feel death ended all things, and VN agreed, just as he had intimated during his entire life in a secret region of his novels. Dmitri, for his part, was struck to find tears in his father's eyes as he kissed VN's forehead on one of their last nights together. When Dmitri softly inquired, his father replied that "a certain butterfly was already on the wing," and something in his glance said he did not believe he would see it again.

*The "Lysandra Cormion," discovered by VN on a serendipitous summer chase.*

A few days later, his breathing weakened to a wheeze. It was an afternoon suffused with light. His wife and son sat by him, looking on, sensing he was aware of their presence to the last. At ten minutes to seven on the evening of Saturday, July 2, 1977, Nabokov groaned three times in descending, operatic resonance. And then, he was gone. When Dmitri, that night, took his mother back to Montreux in his dark-blue racing car, Véra quietly suggested: "Let's rent an airplane and crash."

Nabokov's remains were cremated on a cloudless summer day. The following afternoon, only Véra and Dmitri stood by his grave as his ashes were lowered in an urn, near the Château du Chatelard, in the Clarens cemetery where a great-aunt, Praskovia-Alexandria Nabokov née Tolstoy, also rests. A posthumous homage to VN's fondness for playful schemes of fortune, a Tolstoy and a Nabokov are to be found in the same Swiss cemetery.

Nabokov had not completed *The Original of Laura* and, like Virgil before him, had requested that all traces of the unfinished manuscript be destroyed. In the manner of Virgil's torn executors, however, Véra could not bring herself to burn VN's words. Dmitri, for his part, on revisiting his father's room at the Montreux Palace shortly after his death, would only disclose this much: "There is another, very special box, containing a substantial part of the breathtakingly original *Original of Laura*, which would have been father's most brilliant novel, the most concentrated distillation of his creativity." For more than thirty years, until Dmitri in 2008 took it upon himself to publish them, the fragments of *Laura* would lie in a Swiss vault, its few clandestine readers sworn to secrecy.

. . . . . . . . . . . . . . . . . . . . . . . . . . . . . . . . . . . . . . . . . . . . . . . . . . . . . . . . . . . . .

For the moon never beams, without bringing me dreams . . .

. . . . . . . . . . . . . . . . . . . . . . . . . . . . . . . . . . . . . . . . . . . . . . . . . . . . . . . . . . . . .

Thirty-three years have passed since Nabokov's death—a fair part of which I've spent: devouring VN story after VN story; engaging on a stealthy mission of literary sleuthing; teaching myself a third-rate brand of Russian; doing various other things which, here and there, I shall soon weave into my tale.

For now, on a pale morning in late summer, I am looking out toward Lake Geneva, from the hills above Montreux. I've come to Switzerland to see Dmitri and visit the cemetery at Clarens, where Vladimir's and Véra's ashes have been mixed. When his mother died, Dmitri later told me, it took the gravediggers hours to find the urn where his father's ashes had been placed: "They were something out of Shakespeare." Toward the end of the afternoon, the urn was finally opened. Two handfuls of dust. The modest coda to their fifty-two-year marriage, beyond the finish line of time.

*I do not know if it has ever been noted before that one of the main characteristics of life is discreteness.* I step into the cemetery in a mood of subdued panic. Somehow, standing before its walled recess, I'd imagined Clarens like the Père-Lachaise in Paris, where Oscar Wilde, Marcel Proust, Jim Morrison, and hundreds of others have been assigned numbered graves. Maps detailing the vast crisscross are presented at the entrance, peevish guards patrol day and night, and inscriptions have been carved on eye-catching trees by devoted visitors.

In Clarens, there is nothing. *Unless a film of flesh envelops us, we die. Man exists only insofar as he is separated from his surroundings.* A sea of gravestones is sprawling before me. I am greeted by the hushed morning sigh of tall trees, the isolated pallor of an empty church, the large castle tower that seems sketched into the background. Like Alice lost in a terrific maze, thinking I have traveled all this way in vain, that I have a train to board in just a few hours, that I will never find him, I say a quick, halfhearted prayer. In the distance, a pair of bird wings quiver. *The cranium is a space-traveler's helmet. Stay inside or you perish.* The sky is uncovering a turquoise blue. I make out the curve of a hill. The sun-washed graves shine noiselessly in the cool of this early-September morning. I turn around and glance at the iridescent expanse of Lake Geneva, the delicately cut out slopes eyeing one another on the far end of the horizon. Swiftly zooming back to the task at hand, I pace toward the church and the cemetery's toolshed. "Hello, hello? Anyone there?" *Death is divestment, death is communion.* Miffed, I run to the small crematorium on the right, circling it, sure to find at least a benevolent face, a human pair of eyes. No one. The cemetery is nearly empty.

I walk on, overtaken by this wave of marble slabs, feeling so near yet so absolutely aimless. *It may be wonderful to mix with the landscape, but to do so is the end of the tender ego.* And there, all of a sudden, to my right, I notice a gray-blue gravestone, as plain as any other. (What are the mathematical probabilities, I briefly wonder, of walking past this tomb, unannounced, inconspicuous, among so many thousands?)

On a bare rectangle, I have just glimpsed:

VLADIMIR NABOKOV
ÉCRIVAIN 1899–1977

And right beneath:

VÉRA NABOKOV
1902–1991

I lean down for a moment and lay the palm of my hand on the flecked marble. I think of his hand setting down *The Gift* on paper in that Berlin apartment of the 1930s, I think of the hawkmoths he loved to catch in brown-sugar-and-rum blends on heady August nights in America, the joyousness he experienced at observing their striated wings

between his thumb and forefinger. There is an air of gentle-
ness about this cemetery, an inviting and uncanny note of
calm. *Unless a film of flesh* . . . Very slowly, obsessively, like
a throbbing melody jumbled in a dream, VN's words keep
whirling round and round my head.

. . . . . . . . . . . . . . . . . . . . . . . . . . . . . . . . . . . . . . . . . . . . . . . . . . . . . . . . . . . . .

For the moon never beams,
        without bringing me—

. . . . . . . . . . . . . . . . . . . . . . . . . . . . . . . . . . . . . . . . . . . . . . . . . . . . . . . . . . . . .

Some days earlier, I had, in fact, had a dream. He was
there. So close I could almost touch him. Looking into my
face. His features culled from the countless photographs I
had observed over the years . . . He is standing straight, a
jocular glint in his eye. He appears to be traipsing uphill
on a meadow covered with giant flowers. He is holding an
outlandishly oversized butterfly net. The image is in black
and white. And although he doesn't say a word, his expression exudes curiosity and kindness—which at once imparts
extravagant happiness to the dreamer.

On a late afternoon at Dmitri's, after swallowing
successive slices of pear tart (Madeleine, the cook, looks
as though she has emerged from a backdoor of *Ada*'s Ardis
Hall), toward the end of a long conversation, fearing he
might find it ludicrous, or irritating, I share this image
with Nabokov's son. I have tiptoed into this, expecting
him to brush the dream off as a reader's monomaniacal
fantasy, to discard it as sadly asinine. But to my surprise,

Dmitri is moved, even pleased. His father, still present, sauntering into someone's dream . . . For a sheer instant, his ice-blue eyes seem to well up. I am astonished, as I was the first time he opened the door of his Montreux home, by the physical resemblance between father and son. I see that, as he himself nears the age at which his father's life came to a close, it remains just as impossible to accept that Father is no more. "When a new item clicks into consciousness," Dmitri has written, "my first mental reflex is the thought of bringing it to Father for approval, like a sea-levigated stone on a Riviera beach in childhood; and only a split-pang later do I realize there is no Father. Would he have liked my little offerings?" Fortuitous connections, clues concealed by Fate's wily fingers: a Roman piazza named "Margana" following an accidental anagram, a fang-shaped Swiss mountain called Dent-Favre after the Nabokovs' old Swiss dentist in Massachusetts, or that dilapidated green truck sporting the dubious label "Tooth Transport." And it occurs to me that I too have, once in a while, peered through the lens of a Nabokovian eye. That slinking black cat in Moscow's Patriarch's Pond. The protruding buttocks of Picasso's *Demoiselles d'Avignon* unwittingly matching those of four gaping spectators. My own distorted reflection in a child's red-rimmed sunglasses.

*My idea of VN.*

## CHAPTER 2

# HAPPINESS IN A BRIGHT DOT OF MEMORY

(Where the writer recaptures time and
the reader pulls out a mirror)

hroughout the first pages I heard, not a spurt of laughter, but a sigh:

> The
> cradle rocks above
> an abyss,
> and
> common
> sense tells
> us that
> our
> existence is
> but a brief
> crack of light
> between two eternities
> of darkness . . .

In a far-off recess of memory emerges a dot of light.

It's late summer, 1903. Vladimir, aged four, is ambling down an alley of oaklings in Vyra, the Nabokovs' country estate outside St. Petersburg. As a carpet of green earth unfurls before his eyes, he holds fast, with each frail hand, to a larger and sturdier hand. Through a loophole in time, he appears tucked away, still, in a crease of timelessness where father, mother and child are but one and the same unreal creature, when suddenly he discovers his father is thirty-three and his mother twenty-seven, that they are two not one, and perhaps even three.

It may have been his mother's birthday, in the last, drawling days of August in northern Russia. He remembers the limpid sunlight, the smooth contours of speckles gliding on the surface of shrubs and trees. "I felt myself plunged abruptly into a radiant and mobile medium that was none other than the pure element of time. One shared it—just as excited bathers share shining seawater—with creatures that were not oneself but that were joined to one by time's common flow," VN wrote half-a-century later, in his autobiography, *Speak, Memory*.

Time's pale fire now wheeled the weight of the world, shedding light on the discreteness of things, cracking open the dormer window of consciousness. "Indeed, from my present ridge of remote, isolated, almost uninhabited time, I see my diminutive self as celebrating, on that August day 1903, the birth of sentient life." Time had ushered in consciousness, tipped the hourglass of perception. Time, at this instant, *was* consciousness. An anonymous gift extended onto man "amidst the night of non-being."

Early evenings in Vyra. After his mother had read to him in the candlelight of the drawing room (Vyra's manor, like *Ada*'s Ardis Hall, deliberately shunned electricity), she would gently imply that time had come to travel up the stairs. Dreading the hour of sleep, delaying the ultimate moment, Vladimir would putter about, always reluctant to will himself to bed. Then came the Proustian ritual: His mother would take his hand, "Step, step, step . . ." he remembers her saying, so that Vladimir might walk up the cast-iron staircase with closed eyes. "Step, step, step and I would stumble, you would laugh," he'd recall in a letter to her, fifteen years later. Safely moored to her hand, a three-foot apprentice, he was wrapped in the interior realm of bright particles sweeping through his pupils, staving off the night for just another second.

Following the Nabokovian rule that literature starts, not on the first, but the metaphorical second reading ("curiously enough," he wrote, "one cannot read a book: one can only reread it"), every so often I visualize Vyra with a peculiar clarity, a clarity which likely departs—which, perhaps, must *in essence* depart—from the words inscribed on the page . . .

But who exactly am I?

To begin with, I could tell you that I was born at the tail end of 2,500 years, on the brink of an upheaval that would alter—at least in my own flummoxed eyes—the course of history. I will spare you the details of my infancy, but this much I should say: I grew up in a family expelled from an age locked in a receding ball of glass. "Once upon a time, and such a very different time it was!" became the leitmotiv that rocked my cradle. Though I should also add straight off that a genuine aversion to politics (in which I keenly join VN) precludes me from expanding on the accidents of geography. Suffice it to say that, in the first days of turmoil, my uncle was assassinated. My grandmother unexpectedly passed away. My mother was the final person to be called on the endless waiting list for the last flight out, amidst an airport convulsed with fear. That night, the borders were closed, and from the airplane she saw her country silently withdraw before her eyes. My father and I, by chance, had been away and were never to return.

We'd been fortunate to survive, but a world had dimmed. The end had come, a little more than a year after my birth. And although I can promise you I am neither a pessimist nor a clinical paranoiac, I steadily grew aware of an insidious design of fate: Anything I started seemed to herald the end of something wider and greater. Places I visited, institutions I attended, various characters I came across, all seemed on the verge of decline (or downright oblivion), following a protracted golden age I had just missed, or so it felt, by a jot. As far as personal patterns go—and patterns, you'll see, mattered infinitely to VN—mine was to begin at the end.

So was my obsession with Nabokov a corollary of nostalgia? The particular sense of loss spawned out of a collapsed past? Was it the textured voice of a novelist exiled from both country and native tongue which invited me to dwell in his universe?

In the early years of my adolescence, it was initially a chance encounter with three extraordinary texts. Three books spotted repeatedly on my mother's dark-red brocaded armchairs: *Speak, Memory*; *Ada, or Ardor: A Family Chronicle*; *Lolita, or the Confession of a White Widowed Male*. I knew she had been a sleepless child, reading through the night to wash away her anguish. "Do you like that book?" I'd asked, intrigued by the nude adolescent girl on the cover of *Ada, or Ardor*. "It's one of the most *luminous* novels I've ever read. But it's not for you just yet," she had replied, eliciting rabid curiosity, quelled only by my ignorance of English. I plotted my way to a copy in translation, of course, but the first pages proved entirely forbidding. So that in the end, wait I did, and a good many years. But in the intervening time lapse, she would read aloud and translate for me passages of *Speak, Memory*, which plainly, at times heartrendingly, recalled her own childhood. The forests of blue firs by the sea-lake, the glorious countryside in summertime, her grandparents who time and again had traveled to Russia in the first decade of the twentieth century, in another world which appeared as remote and mysterious to her now as it was to be always unreal to me.

When my turn came to read VN, nostalgia was already one step removed: it had belonged to my mother. My own ears were tuned to the pure enchantment of his prose, which sang to me of languages I knew to be my own. Thus mine were dream-slow reads—weeks, months, spent deciphering one book, meandering into another. Every page, often every sentence, read and reread by a little maniac in the making, wide eyes glowing slightly brighter by the day. Everywhere, it seemed, blossomed sentences so new, yet which one believed to have whispered in a distant fold of time, under some latticed shade.

Visualizing with a peculiar clarity . . . a clarity which likely departs—which, perhaps, must *in essence* depart—from the words inscribed on the page.

Daylight. A Russian afternoon in midsummer. The tennis games in Vyra's new park, circa 1910. A tawny court trapped among towering pine trees. "Play!" Elena Ivanovna, VN's mother, calls out, from her white chalk lining. *"Igraite!"* She rallies in a long dress. She might even be wearing a hat. Her partner, always Vladimir. Mother and favorite son teamed up against Sergey, Vladimir's lanky younger brother, and their father, the liberal statesman Vladimir Dmitrievich Nabokov. Occasionally, Vladimir and Elena quarrel over a weak serve, a missed backhand. Around

*"A bright little gap in the park."*

them, the quivering silence of the park—a formidable echo chamber to the thud of bouncing balls, the footfall of sudden sprints. Their laughter, like heat waves, rippling over the yellows of acacias in bloom. (The entire court, in fact, "A bright little gap in the park, five hundred yards away— or fifty years away from where I am now.")

On a rainy evening, Vladimir bikes over to the edge of Vyra, up the sloping road pointing to the village of Gryazno. His bicycle leaves a track in the transparent shade. His pale feet, bound up in summer sandals, are stained with countless specks of mud. Threads of water run down the nape of his neck. He frowns imperceptibly, slender mouth tightly shut. There is a linden tree on the left side of the path, at the precise location where his father proposed to his mother, in the last years of the nineteenth century. And as he rides past dark pines and clumps of firs, mingling sounds begin to juggle in his mind. Drip. Beam. Drop. Gleam. He bikes past a ramshackle isba, a rusty carriage (horses vanished), and when the rain thickens, he stops for a while under a wooden shelter in the open air. He breathes, his mouth now slightly opened as he takes in the rivulets of water around his feet, the murmur of the park beneath him, the drifting scent of damp cones. Clip clop.

On certain days, when I am not thinking of anything else, when I am waiting for someone to emerge on a side street in a foreign city, when I am traveling across endless expanses of land, when I am on the brink of falling asleep— for just a fraction in time I seem to breathe Vyra's wet earth at the close of that rainy evening. Somehow it is as though I've visited the ancestral park, on the other side of a sentence, in the white sea beyond the black signposts of sense.

A breeze of sunlight. The morning hour lazily pressing on, taking its time. The dining room at Vyra, on the first floor, French windows carved in a pale-green façade, honeysuckle peeking through the porch. The click and clatter of cutlery. A drop of honey oozing down the curve of a blue china bowl like a drowsy caterpillar. Vladimir ladles out another spoonful, and watches the honey as it stretches languidly from airy silver to buttered toast. He will recollect its translucent sheen half-a-century later. The lightheaded happiness of a morning in early life.

*A*
*brief crack*
*of light*
*between*
*two*
*eternities*
*of darkness . . .*

Oh, but "time, so boundless at first blush, was a prison," VN would write. "The prison of time is spherical and without exits." He was a self-styled chronophobiac racing toward the abyss at some 4,500 heartbeats an hour, acutely conscious of standing on the stern of time itself.

However, as time sets off, Vladimir records his mother's gaze on their receding world. "To love with all one's soul and leave the rest to fate . . ." This was to be her gift. " '*Vot zapomni* [now remember]' she would say in conspiratorial tones as she drew my attention to this or that loved thing in Vyra—a lark ascending the curds-and-whey sky of a dull spring day, heat lightning taking pictures of a distant line of trees in the night, the palette of maple leaves on brown sand, a small bird's cuneate footprints on new snow."
Now remember.

## CHAPTER 3

# HAPPINESS, OR AT LEAST A PART OF IT

(Where the writer feels terribly infatuated and the

reader turns out to be something of a sleuth)

n VN's own life, first love would elicit the most vivid flashes of reminiscence.

The girls of *Speak, Memory* . . . There was Zina, "lovely, sun-tanned, bad-tempered" Zina by the ocean in Biarritz. Colette, the nine-year-old beach mate with whom Vladimir eloped, gold coin and butterfly net in hand, to a forbidden cinema. There was a certain American girl, in Berlin, who emerged one evening on roller skates and was at once nicknamed "Louise" though she'd always remain anonymous. (Vladimir's grimace, the night he recognized Louise parading in gaudy props on the stage of a music hall, his reverie of demure solitude trampled.) In Russia, there would be Polenka, the daughter of the head coachman at Vyra, standing by her isba, staring into the sunset, as he whisked past on his bicycle. Never spoken to, always observed from a distance, her image "the first to have the poignant power, by merely *not* letting her smile fade, of burning a hole in my sleep and jolting me into clammy consciousness, whenever I dreamed of her." And the strange afternoon he caught a glimpse of her, naked, cavorting with girlish delight on the banks of the Oredezh, by the old bathhouse. But then—there was Tamara, who turned her predecessors into paltry harbingers. Plump, downy Tamara. Tamara of the Tatar eyes trespassing in the woods of Vyra with two bright-eyed coevals. Tamara, with whom the sixteen-year-old Vladimir, in one particular pine grove, "parted the fabric of fancy . . . tasted reality."

His first glance at her, stolen from a hidden viewpoint, unseen, unrequited. "That hushed July afternoon, when I discovered her standing quite still (only her eyes were moving) in a birch grove, she seemed to have been spontaneously generated there, among those watchful trees, with the silent completeness of a mythological manifestation."

First breath. August 9, 1915, four-thirty.

First memory. Her plenteous dark hair. Though cropped a year later, Vladimir will "always recall it as it looked first, fiercely braided into a thick plait that was looped up at the back of her head and tied there with a big bow of black silk."

Pell-mell. Their trysts in the woods, the lecherous

*"Tamara," or Lyussya Shulgin.*

young tutor who spied on them through the shrubbery, a
protruding telescope giving him away. The delusion of a
hostile winter in St. Petersburg (museum back rooms offer-
ing no substitute for the coppice of Vyra). The last time he
saw her, in the car of a country train, biting into a chocolate
bar. And her final letters, never opened, never read, after
his family's sudden departure from a harbor in southern
Crimea, on a ship bound for Constantinople.

The original Tamara was named Valentina Shulgin,
the girl perched in an apple tree the first day she had ever
caught sight of him. Vladimir called her Lyussya. And as I

read about Lyussya, and the fabulous burst of consciousness she had afforded him, I began to wonder if VN's own
life might not have seeped into his fiction to a far greater
extent than I had ever been willing to believe until then.
Even though I wouldn't quite acknowledge it yet, it appears
obvious to me now that I had, from that moment on, set
out on a journey of literary sleuthing which would one day
bring me to write this book.

For years, I had put off reading *Speak, Memory* in its
entirety. Fiction was the word: *Ada, Lolita, The Gift, Pale
Fire* (in covertly retreating order). To these color-studded
worlds I tenaciously believed the biographical "I" lent
nearly nothing. So who gave a damn about childhood tribulations, adultery, sin everlasting? (Those countless suspi-
cions that bedevil so many to this day . . . Ah the detail, the
lurid, pitch-perfect detail! The lurking true confession!)
Upholding the sovereignty of fiction was, by the end of the
twentieth century, inexpiably passé. Great writers may not
write before they live. As to *Vivian Darkbloom*, this
sorry inventor of true lies, he need only be set straight.
Literature tells the truth. It does not make it up. (But I am
digressing.)

One summer night, as I was walking down a street
of Montreux, I came across a stall of dusty American
books. Out of habit, I casually drew my hand over their
rugged spines and discerned *Speak, Memory*, neatly packed
on the long metallic shelf beside *Lolita* and *Ada*. McFate,
it seemed, meant business. A triangular adolescent pat-

tern had just emerged again. I purchased the book and spent the ensuing days under the seedy arbors of a public garden, my only interruptions a spell of rain or an averted conversation with a local variety of lady-killer. The book I was absorbing was unlike any autobiography I had ever read. An enticing volume composed of 14 chapters and a whimsical appendix, it did not seek to record the steady pulse of a life, or rack up intimate detail for its own tedious sake. *Speak, Memory* was as sensuously appealing as a work of fiction. No hollow monument to the past, but a search into its designs, unseen at first sight, yet stippled, ever so lightly, in the texture of time. It bore witness to life as a creative work-in-progress, unbeknownst to the anxious subject, but caught by the artist's retrospective eye. "The following of such thematic designs through one's life should be, I think, the true purpose of autobiography," Nabokov wrote. *Speak, Memory* stood out in my mind as a singular volume in the libraries of so-called nonfiction—at once a looking glass and a startling lens through which the fixed ideas I'd had, regarding the reflections of literature and life, were slowly being turned on their heads.

"First and last things often tend to have an adolescent note," VN inscribed in the book's opening lines. First and last, a crimson thread. The memory of his first love haunting his compositions to the last.

For here she comes, Lyussya, in her variegated masks, gliding down the glass slides of fiction, never exactly the same, never exactly another. Mashenka, the vanished first love of a disintegrated past. Tamara, stepping into a glade speckled with Camberwell Beauties. Annabel, holding teenage Humbert's "scepter of passion" in a concealed mimosa grove on the French Riviera. Ada, pale and dark-haired, chattering away rapturously on her carbide-lit bicycle, as she pedals into the dusk of Ardis Park. "An adolescent note . . ." Likely it is Lyussya who, recaptured through the versatile prism of memory, inhabits VN's imagination with that abiding glimmer. The vibrato of first things. The round apricot of a glistening mouth. The supple curvature of a thigh. Every time he took her in broad daylight, among the pine shrubs of Vyra. Or else on its adjacent estate along the Oredezh River—Uncle Vasily's manor, under the ancient lime trees of which Vladimir met Lyussya on rainy nights.

Back in St. Petersburg, however, in the spring of 1916, Vladimir perceived, through Lyussya's sharper eyes, that the ardors of their first summer would never be rekindled. He had written, in homage to his curvy muse, stacks of maudlin poems, a selection of which had been published in St. Petersburg at his own expense. Yet no sooner had Lyussya read them than she noticed a nagging detail which had escaped him. "There it was, the same

ominous flaw, the banal hollow note, and glib suggestion
that our love was doomed since it could never recapture
the miracle of its initial moments, the rustle and rush
of those limes in the rain, the compassion of the wild
countryside."

The preceding winter in the city had opened unto a
pale and dwindling world, which later viewed through the
long lens of exile, would in turn seem like a lucid rem-
nant of that first summer, resonating still with the sustained rumor of lost things. A copper streak of sunshine in
the late afternoon; a peal of adolescent laughter; a white-
washed column in Uncle Vasily's manor (that very last one,
all the way to the left); a voluble river, overheard during a
solitary foray in the birch woods of old Russia; an outdoor
banquet in an alley of blue firs; a fairytale picnic at which
the children arrive in a charabanc; and "the rapture of her
identity."


Fast forward and still. The first summers of fiction.

As I was writing the preceding paragraph, I started to
recall some of the first lines of *Lolita*: "There might have
been no Lolita at all had I not loved, one summer, a certain initial girl-child. In a princedom by the sea." Annabel,
the primeval Lolita of Humbert's life. The dead girl-child
whom this Dolly Haze, caught twenty-four years later sun-
bathing in the grass, summons back in a gasp. "And then,
without the least warning, a blue sea-wave swelled under

my heart and, from a mat in a pool of sun, half-naked, kneeling, turning about on her knees, there was my Riviera love peering at me over dark glasses." Twenty-four years obliterated by a ruse of time.

I recalled the first day Van sets his eyes on Ada. She is but a "dark-haired girl of eleven or twelve," stepping out of a horse carriage with her mother, by the entrance door to Ardis Hall. His first image of Ada (or rather the way he will remember her, holding freshly picked flowers): "She wore a white frock with a black jacket and there was a white bow in her long hair. He never saw that dress again and when he mentioned it in retrospective evocation she invariably retorted that he must have dreamt it, she never had one like that, never could have put on a dark blazer on such a hot day, but he stuck to his initial image of her to the last." That first memory, blatantly real, or dreamily distorted, fixed to the very last in Van's fancy.


I do not believe VN's novels are the transcripts of his past, but they do recapture the enduring light of that first summer. That unique burst of consciousness which continued to reverberate throughout his life. Like filaments of memories coalescing in unforeseen clusters, where happiness— or at least a part of it—is a variation on remembrance.

*Experiencing happiness.*

## CHAPTER 4

# A BURST OF HAPPINESS

(Where the writer talks about the only real thing in
the world and the reader becomes quite talkative)

 *onsciousness is the only real thing in the world and the greatest mystery of all!*

It's a mesh of light in a mantle of darkness, a twinned iris; an Eve of flesh and dust; a thrush singing over the gray of a November morning; a glint of laughter tearing the fabric of night; a ghostly skiff on pale-green waters; the minute symmetry of a snowflake.

*How small the cosmos (a kangaroo's pouch would hold it), how paltry and puny in comparison to human consciousness, to a single individual recollection and its expression in words . . .*

. . . to the whiteness of a man's teeth rotting in a pool of blood; to the damp smell of a late summer sky; to a bubble of sunshine glistening in a brass knob; to the tawny hind-wing of a Tiger Moth; to a widening

pupil in half-light; to a wisp of crimson cracked open
at dawn; to the lee-side of sleep.

*Consciousness is a message scribbled in the dark.*

It's a dent of light; a firefly pursuing darkness like a
dream; the glow of an amethyst on translucent skin;
a handful of shimmering sand; a sliver of anguish;
the stridence of cut glass; time made I.

*That sudden window swinging open on a sunlit
landscape . . .*

. . . a Spring Azure fretting in mid-flight; a gallery
of see-through mirrors; a mad poet's magic carpet;
words giving rise to live creatures; the whisper of
swelling water; a lantern leaning against the night;
eyes sooty and sea green; the pang of agony in a
needlepoint of light.

All the world is but *a universe embraced by consciousness.
The arms of consciousness reach out and grope, and the longer they are the better.*

## CHAPTER 5

# A SUMMARY OF SIX MAD HATTERS' HAPPINESS

(Where the writer and others fall madly in love
and the reader falls asleep)

ove—the claire-obscure arabesque of the Nabokovian universe.

Yet alas, all happy lovers are more or less dissimilar; all unhappy ones are more or less alike. (I am parodying not one, but two great Russian writers.)

In VN's eyes, happiness in love calls for unconditional singularity. So that in the three following stories, real or imaginary, you may catch the rarest clues to *peculiar happiness* in italics.

## LEGALLY MAD LOVE

After Zina, Colette, Louise, Polenka, and Lyussya faded in the dusk of his boyhood, on the fast streets of Petersburg and Berlin, Vladimir "entered an extravagant phase of sentiment and sensuality," during which he appeared as "a hundred different young men at once, all pursuing one changeful girl in a series of simultaneous or overlapping love affairs . . . , with very meager artistic results."

But on the night of May 8, 1923, Vladimir stepped toward a woman named Véra Evseevna Slonim, on a bridge in Berlin. It was she who had invited him to join her on that bridge. She donned a black mask, admired his poetry, had memorized his verse. He likely had never seen her face and in hopeful wonder observed the wolflike profile of her mask emerge from that darkness.

In the spring of 1925, he married her and soon praised the "radiant truthfulness" of nuptial love in a letter to his sister Elena. In 1937, he had an affair in Paris with a White Russian beauty who anxiously sought to marry him. Quite unlike the sexed creatures of his novels, however, the "bird of paradise" of Russian émigré literature suffered a dreadful episode of psoriasis, and even contemplated suicide. Véra received an anonymous letter denouncing the affair. If he had fallen in love, she told him, he should leave. Perhaps he had. But leave he did not. In fact, from then on they barely ever left one another.

Volodya, as she knew him, loved Véra's uncanny memory, her marvelously exact Russian. He reveled in her arch sense of humor. She was his idea "to the x degree" of the feminine. Though she had briefly translated Poe, she was not in the business of translation; he, for his part, was "frankly homosexual on the subject of translators." She had

never harbored literary ambitions of her own; he thought
absolutely nothing of "lady writers." (What he might have
thought of a perilously Nabokovian would-be writer of the
feminine gender, I shudder to imagine.) After they were
married, Véra, a relentless filer of her husband's work,
never saved a single page of the translations she had published in her youth. (Might she have written anything herself had she not married Vladimir Nabokov? I suppose that
is beside the point.) "The sharpest jealousy of all," VN had
written in the letter informing his family he would marry
her, "is that between one woman and another, and that
between one littérateur and another. But when a woman
envies a littérateur, that can amount to $H_2SO_4$ [sulfuric
acid]." Suffice it to say, Véra regarded her husband, with
steadfast conviction, as the greatest writer of his time.
Thus (for it must have been a "thus") happily she played the
part of:

WIFE

LOVER

MINDER

READER

ASSISTANT

TYPIST

AGENT

CHAUFFEUR

BODYGUARD

CHESS PARTNER

PRIVATE BANKER

PRACTICAL GENIUS, ETC.

In America, she acquired a Browning .38 which she was licensed to fire and stored in a brown box. She was cautious and secretive. Discreet and sophisticated. She had a striking aura, her prematurely white hair glowing as it were on her ageless features.

Rather graciously, VN dedicated most of his novels to Véra. "And her picture has often been reproduced by some mysterious means of reflected color in the inner mirrors of my books." But his model she was not. In 1958, when she traveled with her husband on *Lolita*'s publicity tour, a headline reckoned, "Madame Nabokov is 38 Years Older than the Nymphet Lolita." (Véra, incidentally, had saved the draft of *Lolita* as Nabokov set out to hurl it in their garden incinerator: "We are keeping this," she'd said.)

No matter, she remained the object of bizarre speculation, in turn cover-up, counterpoint, or mannequin. "I do get annoyed when people I never met impinge on my privacy with false and vulgar assumptions—as for example Mr. Updike, who in an otherwise clever article absurdly suggests that my fictional character, bitchy and lewd Ada, is, I quote, 'in a dimension or two, Nabokov's wife.' " To Matthew Hodgart, following a review in the *New York Times*, VN replied: "What the hell, Sir, do you know about my married life?"

Marriage, for the Nabokovs, was a sealed sanctuary sus-

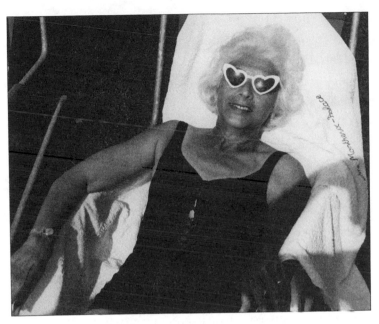

*12 + 38.*

pended above the abyss of eternity. A phalanx of two. An
invisible hyphen weaving his every word, appearing, somehow, when you least expected it. For of a sudden, there she
was, in her translucent mask, riding along the quiet crease
of a line, the hushed "you" of *Speak, Memory*, lightly surfac-
ing at the turn of a sentence, in the fifteenth and last chapter: *"Posthaste, posthaste . . . the years are passing,
my dear, and presently nobody will know what you
and I know."* His waypoint of silence.

In 1961, the Nabokovs moved to the Montreux Palace
Hotel, in Switzerland.

We know nothing of their private lives. Except that they slept in adjoining rooms. Perhaps he tiptoed to hers. And late into the night, he would look at her, lying naked, supine, gray-blue eyes lifted skyward. Then soundlessly, he would again disappear in the dark haze of his room.

We know of their dreams. Like the twin dreamers of *Ulysses*, now and then the Nabokovs dreamed alike. "It has been suggested by doctors that we sometimes pooled our minds when we dreamed," he wrote in a story. And he also believed, as Van Veen would formulate it a few years later, in the "precognitive flavor" of dreams. (There, among variegated shades, we might perceive the future, "catch sight of the lining of time.") Over several months, VN recorded and labeled his dreams, as he might have pinned bewildered butterflies—Russian, cataclysmic, erotic, literary, precognitive. Véra's dreams were grained with mute anxieties. She dreamed of forbidden frontiers and barefoot escapes (her son clasped against her chest). Or else she slipped slowly through the wooden staves of the floor loosening under her step.

On a winter night in November 1964, together they dreamed of the Soviet uprising.

In a letter to Véra that same year, Vladimir had written: "You know, we are awfully like one another. In letters, for example: We both love to (1) unobtrusively insert foreign words, (2) quote from our favorite books, (3) translate our impressions from one sense (sense of sight, for example) into impressions of another sense (sense of taste, for

*He and You.*

example), (4) ask forgiveness at the end for some imaginary nonsense, and in many other ways."

## LOPSIDEDLY MAD LOVE

I recall a Mediterranean countryside over a decade ago. The long silhouette of a cypress tree extended its back against the wall of our red-brick house, vying until noon with the prickly stems of caper berry shrubs. After short, stormy nights, scattered pools formed crevasses in the grass. Light reflected off the water like slippery scales. I was sitting down on a white wicker chair, studiously wading through *Lolita* for the first time. I lay still in my washed-out red bathing suit, while my mother's cousin (a versatile double of VN), palette in hand, eyes just slightly open, drew a watercolor of that morning. The drawing vanished several years later, but what remains today, let loose on the pages of my *Lolita*, are stains of suntan lotion and a maze of circles betraying the number of English words I did not know. Vexing as they were, those words, they shone on the page like clues planted by a sly illusionist who murmured in my ear that unfold his magic carpet he would, as soon as I lifted that dictionary slumped idly on the grass.

But the sun was moving up to meet the earth in the eyes, and when it reached its zenith, I dozed off under the growing heat . . . *Lalita Lili Lilita Lilola Lilota Litola Lola Lolita Loll Lolla Lollapalooza Lollipop Lollop Lolly Lollylag Lollypop* . . . In the semi-awareness of dreams in daylight, the *li*'s and *la*'s melded with the low hum of a wasp drowning in a glass, just as my own chair started tipping forward in slow motion. And off I slipped into . . .

Once upon a time, there was a russet girl-child "smelling of orchards in nymphetland." In a mossy garden she lived, among pubescent maidens. She had, alongside various other virtues, a downy nape, a shrill voice and a primitive vocabulary: " 'revolting,' 'super,' 'luscious,' 'goon.' "

When a "big handsome hunk of movieland manhood" moved into her mother's house, she grew ineffably curious, and mildly infatuated. A listless Eve, she spread one leg across his lap, smiled in metallic twinkles, sank her teeth into a crimson apple.

And oh did old Humbert Humbert love his Lo, his Lola, his lovely Dolores Haze, from that glorious first morning, as she lay on her carpet of grass, in her sea of sunshine. His recaptured teenage love, redeeming every other. Forever his love, in that bright shell, coiled on the morning grass, forever shivering in his veins.

For soon, so soon, she would no longer be a girleen. Her breasts and buttocks would flare, her tender features bulge. (Transmogrified!) She'd be plain Dolores Haze, and not just on the dotted line. In this grisly hourglass, doomed she was. "She would be thirteen on January 1. In two years or so she would cease being a nymphet and would turn into a 'young girl,' and then, into a 'college girl'—that horror of horrors."

Was he but a fiendish freak? "We are not sex fiends! Emphatically, no killers are we. Poets never kill," he pleaded, a sardonic smile zipping open behind the page like the transient grin of a Cheshire cat. Proudly, Humbert claimed an Old World lineage of noble men fallen "madly in love." Dante with his Beatrice (nine years old), "a sparkling girleen . . . in a crimson frock, and this was in 1274,

in Florence, at a private feast in the merry month of May."
Petrarch with his Laureen (Lo's fourteenth-century twin),
"a fair-haired nymphet of twelve running in the wind, in
the pollen and dust, a flower in flight, in the beautiful plain
as descried from the hills of Vaucluse."

To make a long story a little terse, Humbert married
Lolita's mother, for pressing and pragmatic reasons. She
was run over by a car on a rainy afternoon. So Humbert had
only to fetch Lolita at camp. Yet mind the twist, it was not
he who seduced her, but she who seduced him, at six-fifteen
in the morning, to be precise, at the Enchanted Hunters
Hotel. She had learned a thing or two at camp. He would
never have imagined it (not so soon at least), but lo and
behold, she'd whispered the idea in his red-hot ear. And in
a glancing moment, they were "technically lovers."

From motel to motel, they traveled cross-country.
(Champion, Colorado! Phoenix, Arizona! Burns, Ore-
gon!) He schemed and dreamed. He loved her frantically.
While she, the elfin child, would be "cruel and crafty"
with "desperate, dying Humbert," so prone to spells of
"despair and desperate meditation." She was moody. She
pinched him. She struck him with a shoe tree. She negoti-
ated his every key to her dazzling paradise. He got her field
glasses and funnies, Cokes and a transparent raincoat. But
to his "wonderland," or better say, his "Humberland," she
preferred "the corniest movies, the most cloying fudge."
Worse yet, "between a Hamburger and a Humburger, she
would—invariably, with icy precision—plump for the

former. There is nothing more atrociously cruel than an adored child."

They'd have it out. She would scream and swear and cry. On certain glacial nights, "icebergs in paradise," he'd be overcome with "the remorse, the poignant sweetness of sobbing atonement, groveling love, the hopelessness of sensual reconciliation." He would lavish avuncular kisses. Caress her yellowish feet. Lick her salty lashes. Lull her to sleep. "I loved you. I was a pentapod monster, but I loved you. I was despicable and brutal, and turpid, and everything, *mais je t'aimais, je t'aimais!* And there were times when I knew how you felt, and it was hell to know it, my little one. Lolita girl, brave Dolly Schiller."

But Lolita was playing a twofold game. She had a second lover who trailed them like a phantom on the treacherous road. A cunning double, he planted shadowy clues on motel registers: "Will Brown, Dolores, Colo.," "Harold Haze, Tombstone, Arizona," "Ted Hunter, Cane, NH." Until on a fatal day, Humbert's archrival swooped and wrested his Carmen away.

Three years passed. Humbert wallowed in agony. Then one morning, he received a letter from Dolly Schiller, now married and pregnant and asking for a handful of money. Swiftly, he drove up to her shack in Coalmont. Slowly, she opened the door . . . "And there she was with her ruined looks and her adult, rope-veined narrow hands and her goose-flesh white arms, and her shallow ears, and her unkempt armpits, there she was (my Lolita!), hopelessly worn at seventeen . . . *and I looked and looked at her, and knew as clearly as I know I am to die, that I loved her more than anything I had ever seen or imagined on earth, or hoped for anywhere else.*"

There it is, the lovely, wretched, medullar music of enduring (and lopsided) passion.

The story ends with a rather literal instance of poetic justice (vengeance is exacted by Humbert upon his protean rival), and some raving lines of stark tenderness written by the criminal in his detention ward. "Lolita, light of my life, fire of my loins. My sin, my soul."

The prefatory note by one Dr. John Ray, Jr., Ph.D., had duly warned us. Lolita died in childbed. All marriages a sham and all wives throttled, only a nymph remains. Lolita alone. Mailed in a madman's coat of words.

# LETHALLY MAD LOVE

"*Lolita* has no moral in tow," Nabokov declared unequivocally. In the convex mirror of novels, he ardently believed, no moral is ever to be gleaned. No lessons are to be learned. A work of literature is a maniac's masterpiece, spine-tingling art at play, a recreated Eden where God no longer lives and primeval love is allowed. At heart, VN wrote, fiction exists "only insofar as it affords me what I shall bluntly call aesthetic bliss, that is a sense of being somehow, somewhere, connected with other states of being where art

(curiosity, tenderness, kindness, ecstasy) is the norm."
What truly matters is the bliss of sensing and seeing—a
naked foot pressed into damp grass, a green snake coiled
round a washbasin, a mouth bent over a lover's detailed
desire.

When I read my second VN novel, *Ada* (quite unevent-
fully, in bed, toes splayed, limbs akimbo), every so often I
put the book down and strove to visualize its figures of light
and shade.

This is the story I saw, and heard.

Ada. Van. Vaniada. Nirvana. "*Da*," the Russian "Yes," whispered that first summer in the arbors of Ardis Park. The
bliss of *da*, contained in Ada, pronounced "the Russian way
with two deep, dark 'a's." The adolescent wonder of Van and
Ada having sex in the candle-haze of the drawing room, the
night of the Burning Barn, when the entire family has sped
away. Van and Ada, fourteen and twelve respectively. First
cousins soon to be siblings, children of Demon and Marina,
on a twin planet named Antiterra. ("INCEST!" the letters
had fatefully turned up in a game of Flavita.)

In his dawn days with precocious Ada, Van had felt "a
void of light and a veil of shade that no force could overcome and pierce." On the nether side of this void lay his
pale cousin's "voluptuous, impermissible skin . . . her angular movements, her gazelle-grass odor, the sudden black
stare of her wide-set eyes, and the rustic nudity under her

dress," so perfectly alien, so fondly familiar. A reflection of slender fingers, a miraculous symmetry of birthmarks . . . How he craved her! And dreamed of touching the rippling mirror, her native strangeness.

Of course, seduce his Ada he did. In attics and arbors, he tasted his sin, his soul and his sibling. In groves and alcoves, on carpets and lap robes, he sought to sate the itch for his demonic twin. And time skipped a quivering pulse, "reality" was forfeited. "It would not be sufficient to say that in his love-making with Ada he discovered the pang, the *ogon'*, the agony of supreme 'reality.' Reality, better say, lost the quotes it wore like claws . . . For one spasm or two, he was safe. The new naked reality needed no tentacle or anchor; it lasted a moment, but could be repeated as often as he and she were physically able to make love." No longer the fact and matter of unfolding days, babble and habit, but a higher plane of reality, informed by Ada's unearthly essence.

Yet in the gardens of Van and Ada's beatitudes, in the "orchards and orchidariums" of Ardis, in the apple-green paradise where "even eccentric police officers grew enamored with the glamour of incest," only a shadow loomed. A red-haired girl, a peevish child, a whimpering half-sister, three years Ada's junior.

The Veen sisters, in faint ways, looked alike: "In both sisters, the front teeth were a trifle too large and the nether lip too fat for the ideal beauty of marble death; and because their noses were permanently stuffed, both girls (especially later, at fifteen and twelve) looked a little dreamy and dazed in profile." Unlike "darkly flossed" Ada, however, Lucette's armpits "showed a slight stipple of bright floss and her chub was dusted with copper."

Anything fiery Ada tasted, Lucette fiercely lusted after. So naturally, poor Lucette, "a macédoine of intuition, stupidity, naïveté and cunning," fell madly in love with Van "the irresistible rake," incidentally her half-brother. Since Van and Ada's first summer days at Ardis Hall, she slinked, she suspected, she compulsively spied. She trotted and trailed and drummed at closed doors. With a skipping rope, they tied her up to a tree and disappeared into the shrubbery. They put her in a bathtub and stole an instant in the pantry. They coaxed her into learning poetry and tiptoed to the nursery. "We are watched by Lucette, whom I shall strangle some day," Ada declared preemptively. Soon, Lucette became a quavering shadow, a green iris eyeing their every tryst.

She was, at times, allowed in their games, but only in part. Ada and she kissed Van under a tree. In turn, the pet was petted, and Ada made love to her Lucile when Van traveled away. (The biological conundrum of "incest," let it be noted, was solved as such: Van was "absolutely sterile despite his prowesses." And Ada freely drank from the filter of "pure joyousness and Arcadian innocence.")

Several years went by, the children grew up.

Lucette, now a *jeune fille*, forever a *demi-vierge* ("half *poule*, half *puella*"), still loved Van desperately: "I adore (*obozhayu*), I adore, I adore, I adore more than life you, you (*tebya, tebya*), I ache for you unbearably (*ya toskuyu po tebe nevïnosimo*)." Van stroked her "apricot-bloomed forearm." But he would not *have* Lucette. Though he professed to admire her, to regard her as a green "bird of paradise." She trembled with rage. "I want Van," she cried, "and not intangible admiration——" "Intangible? You goose. You may gauge it, you may brush it once very lightly, with the knuckles of your gloved hand. I said knuckles. I said once. That will do. I can't kiss you. Not even your burning face. Good-bye, pet."

They did make love, so to speak, one sultry night in Manhattan, all together. Mostly, it was Ada and Van who caressed their fox-red sister. "The fire of Lucette's amber runs through the night of Ada's odor and ardor, and stops at the threshold of Van's lavender goat. Ten, eager, evil, loving, long fingers, belonging to two different young demons caress their helpless bed pet." Lucette pined and panted, but she would not be allowed into Eden. She was the aching bird doomed to overlook their garden. The lone green-eyed creature cast away from sibling bliss.

One last crystal-blue night, on board a transatlantic liner, Lucette declared her love to Van. She did like Dutch and Flemish painting, she said, flowers, food, Shakespeare, and shopping, but all it really came to was a piercing "*tonen'kiy-tonen'kiy* (thin little) layer" under which only Van's image gleamed in the emptiness. That night, she killed herself, jumping off her ocean liner after a final attempt at seducing her half-brother. "At every slap and splash of cold white salt, she heaved with anise-flavored nausea and there was an increasing number, okay, numbness, in her neck and arms. As she began losing track of herself, she thought it proper to inform a series of receding Lucettes—telling them to pass it on and on in a trick-crystal regression—that what death amounted to was only a more complete assortment of the infinite fractions of solitude."

Ada and Van were swept in passing darkness. Ada said she did not know, indeed could not know, that such unhappiness existed at Ardis. By then, Demon, father of Van and Ada Veen, had uncovered the tangles of incest. She had confessed. He had confessed. *("All in all, I suppose I have had her about a thousand times. She is my whole life.")* She had married an Arizonian cattle-breeder. He had slept with every prostitute in every *floramour* on Antiterra. They had sworn to their father they would not meet again. But of course, following his death and Lucile's, they met again. They loved each other still. In fact, they loved each other more, and those days formed "the highest ridge of their twenty-one-year-old love: its complicated, dangerous, ineffably radiant coming of age."

Far later in life, on a fall morning, widowed Ada exclaimed to crotchety old Van, now ninety-seven and contorted with pain (awaiting his morphine shot): "Oh, Van, oh Van, we did not love her enough. *That's* whom you should have married, the one sitting feet up, in ballerina black, on the stone balustrade, and then everything would have been alright—I would have stayed with you both in Ardis Hall, and instead of that happiness, handed out gratis, instead of all that we *teased* her to death!" The blush of paradise, the absolution of darkness and regret, lay beneath the latticed gallery of Ardis, and they did not *know* it in full. But now— in the "glittering 'now' "—their happiness soared against the backdrop of their most agonizing hour. And with this green shadow in the painting, with the cruelty inherent, perhaps, to all mad lovers' towering happiness, Ada and Van retreat into their own extraordinary love lasting nearly a century, "into the finished book, into Eden or Hades, into the prose of the book or the poetry of its blurb."

## CHAPTER 6

# HAPPINESS ACROSS A TRANSPARENT ABYSS

(Where the writer loses all he ever had and the reader goes off on a tangent)

n a languid evening in Montreux, Dmitri sat on the terrace of his home, staring into the shimmer of Lake Geneva, his features unusually stern, his eyes dimming to a dark blue. As he does now and then, he referred to his father as "Nabokov" (pronounce Russian-style: Na-BOAK-off). "What were the three great losses of Na-BOAK-off?" he asked in a stentorian tone. The sun was about to slip into the lake, and the last coots of the day whimpered faintly as they hovered over the vanishing horizon. Quietly seated by Dmitri's side, I was trying to record the last details of that sunset, with the unease that steals into me whenever I gaze at a magnificent landscape or a sumptuous painting. It's a sense of oppression, of helplessness, as though I were called on to draw a precise and impossible summary of beauty. I want to grasp it in one fell

swoop, seize its colors, meld with its texture. So I look, and look, and feel entirely shut out until, once in a while— unforeseeably, blessedly—I am welcomed into that concord. Its exacting beauty "an island of happiness in the clear north of my being."

But even as I am drifting off, leaving the lakeside vista and the melting sun to my own unraveling thoughts (must read "Details of a Sunset" . . . was that a Russian sunset? Swiss sunsets and blue swans appear at the end of *Ada* . . . was this lake any different half-a-century ago? did VN ever travel to its farthest shore? or could that be an island, right there, in the middle, brimming with its own butterflies and plantlets? how I wish I could know all their names and tell apart every caterpillar and plant juice and . . . ), on the far left I suddenly hear Dmitri's basso startling me back to the moment.

## BOYHOOD!

Aboard a ship called *Hope* transporting a cargo of dried fruit, days before turning twenty, in April 1919, Vladimir had escaped Russia. Father and son played a defiant game of chess on the deck as the Bolsheviks fired from the coast and the vessel tremulously made its way to a cold blue sea. The Nabokovs were not allowed to alight in Constantinople and landed in Athens instead. Vladimir would not see Russia again. ("Tamara, Russia, the wildwood grading into old gardens . . . the sight of my mother getting down on her hands and knees to kiss the earth every time we came back to the country from town for the summer, *et la montagne et le grand chêne.*" A childhood, one morning, blithely tossed to sea.) After Athens, there would be London, Berlin, and Cambridge University, where he'd translate one of his most beloved English books, *Alice in Wonderland*, into *Anya v strane chudes.* Then again there'd be a Berlin he never loved, and where he would live as an exile for fourteen-and-a-half years, never fully learning the German language. Through it all, he would remain under the powerful spell of northern Russia, imaginary expeditions, silver birches, misty swamps, and boreal butterflies.


## FATHER!


Three years after the family's flight from Russia, Vladimir's father was killed in a botched assassination by a member of the tsarist extreme right. At a political rally of liberal White Russians, Vladimir Dmitrievich had leaped heroically to prevent the gunman from shooting his target and was murdered in the fray. That night would seal the end of VN's youth. In their apartment in Berlin, he had been reading verses of Blok to his mother —verses likening Florence to "a smoky iris"—when the phone rang. A car tore through the darkness. Vladimir and his mother saw the city disappear before their eyes. They arrived at the hall. His mother screamed a quiet scream, *"Bozhe moy . . .* How can it be?" Hours earlier, on a morning train, Vladimir had traced with his finger the word H A P P I N E S S on the fog of a carriage window. He had watched the letters slither down the glass. His father would be buried in Berlin. "Father is no more," he noted in his diary.

## RUSSIAN!

In 1938, now living in a small apartment in Paris, Nabokov wrote his first novel in English, *The Real Life of Sebastian Knight*, experiencing a peculiar sort of pain. He was leaving his "untrammeled, rich, and infinitely docile Russian tongue for a second-rate brand of English." This was to be his "private tragedy." He requested that an American woman, Lucie Léon Noel, a close friend of Joyce's, correct his manuscript and look over syntax and idioms. They worked on the very table her husband had leaned over with Joyce on *Finnegans Wake*. "Most of it read amazingly smoothly," Lucie would later report. But Nabokov still held two Russian works in his mind, believing he would surely return to the native language he had tuned to lucid precision at the exact time he chose to give it up. A few years later, however, on the loss of Russian he would write English verse:

> *. . . liquid verbs in* ahla *and in* ili,
> *Aonian grottoes, nights in the Altai,*

*Black pools of sound with "l"s for water lilies.*
*The empty glass I touched is tinkling still,*
*But now 'tis covered by a hand and dies . . .*

And in one simile, he likened the daze of the linguistic switch to "moving from one darkened house to another on a starless night."

I often think of this pain. The solitude which in those years must have run through the pulse of VN's writing hand, through his lightest youthful lines. Dmitri speaks of it, at times. Bashfully yielding details of a world which emerges in a trail of ellipses. The jangling melody of the German years, the gray winters so remote from those he had known in his boyhood, the uncertainties of a life no longer foretold.

But then, there was also the grace with which he turned his eyes onto things, gazed so precisely, demanded happiness.

A few other images of VN in Berlin have stayed with me like queer rough cuts of a silent film.

He tried to work in a bank but lasted only three hours. He tutored French, English, and Russian, never a minute beyond the hour. He wrote a Russian grammar. Its first exercise: *Madam, ya doktor, vot banan* ("Madam, I am the doctor, here is a banana"). He gave tennis and boxing lessons. He was handsome and slim. He acted as a nameless extra in a German film. He was Sirin in his byline. Volodya in his trunks. He revised *Invitation to a Beheading* in violet ink. When he wrote, he never read the papers, just books. He never bought any books. He read them standing up in bookstores. He saw Kafka on a tram (or so he thought years later, when he chanced upon a photo of "those most extraordinary eyes"). He was poor, very poor. He asked a literary acquaintance to recommend him:

*A . . . author (embellish)*
*talented!! The pride of the emigration!!*
*New Style!!*
*Grant or fellowship*

Other shots of the same period: VN in worn-out trousers. VN pleading for work, saying he'll move anywhere, Canada, India, South Africa! VN receiving twenty dollars from the Russian Literary Fund in the United States. VN joyously taking part in rural labor in the south of France. VN dining with Russian sailors at the port of Marseille. VN meeting Joyce at supper in Paris and making a dreary impression. VN writing *The Real Life* on a suitcase placed on a bidet in a rusty Parisian bathroom.

"Those most extraordinary eyes . . ." Kafka's, but also his own. I became obsessed with imagining those eyes, VN's staring into Kafka's. And what those two glances (stippled

*Rural laborer.*

amber, pitch black), briefly crossing on that unlikely afternoon, might have expressed.

My own maternal grandparents had lived in Europe
before the war, during those same years. In a mirror
reflection: Paris first, then Berlin, roughly 1923 to 1939.
And as I tried to visualize VN's features in those German
years, I began to consider if perchance, circa 1935, just as
he himself had fancied seeing Kafka on a tram, my curious grandmother, restlessly wandering about town, might

not have caught a glimpse of the young Nabokov. I liked to picture her walking in the black-and-white Berlin of pre-war years, with that lid of dark lead hanging over the city roofs. Though she is alone, she is not afraid (or at least this is what she tells herself). On a day in late winter, she is sauntering in low-crouched streets, the windows a succession of opaque frames behind which she must sense, here and there, the dark gleam of a human presence. She watches the sky moments before the lanterns are lit, as the clouds dissolve, mother-of-pearl drawing slowly on ash. While the night closes in, she starts walking faster, her steps quick, almost shuffling on the blacktop, when at the turn of a street she discerns a tiny door and a window—an artisan's atelier, or a dilapidated shop. A young man, gaunt limbs, forehead leaning toward the glass, amber eyes, is peering through the window at items she cannot tell apart. And what attracts her attention is the eeriness of his gaze, its diffuse wonder, reaching into its own reflection, yet a world removed. A flicker of amber in this engulfing grayness.

Weeks after having completed these lines, with a little pounce of the heart, I came across this paragraph in VN's all-but-forgotten essay, *Nikolaï Gogol*:

> *We dream sometimes of perfectly unimportant people, a chance*
> *fellow traveler or such like dim person whom we met years ago*

*and never saw again. One may thus imagine a retired business man in the Boston of 1875, casually telling his wife of having dreamt the other night that together with a young Russian or Pole whom he had once met in Germany when he was young himself he was buying a clock and a cloak in a shop of antiques.*

Back to Germany, where the rest of this reel uncoils. VN had fallen in love with Véra in Berlin and married her in 1925. They'd struggled in very narrow quarters, especially after Dmitri's birth in 1934. VN worried about the next day's earnings. And the political situation was ominous. Véra was Jewish, and after the Nazis won over the German parliament in 1932, it became exceedingly difficult to obtain émigré passports. To the Nabokovs' dismay, in the spring of 1936, by a blow of fate, the reviled General Biskupsky was named head of Hitler's Department for Russian Émigré Affairs. He appointed as his undersecretary Sergey Taboritsky, the man convicted of murdering VN's father.

As fast as possible, VN moved to France, to seek work. Véra and Dmitri joined him in the summer of 1937. While the war began raging on the eastern border, the family escaped in May 1940 with funding from a Jewish rescue organization. Within days, German tanks rolled into the French capital. VN had left papers, two manuscripts, and a splendid set of European butterflies in a basement that was rifled by the Germans after his departure. His pages, scattered on the pavement, were saved by a Jewish woman whose uncle, a close friend of the Nabokovs, would die in a

Émigré passport, April 1940.

concentration camp. Three weeks later, the entire building was pulverized.

In the nick of time, VN was hired to teach writing at Stanford, and the Nabokovs sailed to the United States on board the SS *Champlain*. They were originally booked to travel on the ship's later voyage, but obtained, by chance, a last set of earlier tickets. On its following journey, the *Champlain* was torpedoed by a U-boat and sunk at sea. In a span of exactly twenty years, VN had escaped both the Bolsheviks and the Nazis by a fortuitous turn of events. But his mother had died in Prague in 1939, and VN had not been by her side. By the time he managed to save his wife and son from the brown tide overtaking Europe, Czechoslovakia had long been locked into Nazi lines. And Nabokov had yet to lose his younger brother, Sergey, who was outspokenly homosexual and would perish in a German camp of starvation and exhaustion.

Crimea, Berlin, Paris, the flight West to America. This was a time when life was elsewhere. When history's currents pulled frantically, making all but nothing of freewill. In time, however, exile would provide VN with a "syncopal kick" he "would not have missed for worlds." Distance, the destruction of things past, a childhood secured like snowflakes adrift in a sphere of glass . . . Looking back to his northern city, he found it teeming with more shades than he had ever observed in his youth. "Homesickness has been with me a sensuous and particular matter." Homesickness would weave the iridescent texture of his prose: a skein of limber threads, one yarn always concealing another, farther, dreamier thread.

Years before, Vladimir's homesickness had been set off by the family's move to Gaspra, in southern Crimea, where nothing seemed quite Russian anymore. The blue village minaret, the "karakuls of the dark Tauric pines," the "positively Baghdadian" donkey braying in unison with the evening chants of the muezzin, had provoked Vladimir's first throes of nostalgia. There had been harbingers in his childhood too, the months he had spent away from Vyra, in Biarritz or Berlin. But the sensation had been magnified in Crimea, where the image of Lyussya Shulgin, her letters, *her* nostalgia for Vyra, weighed heavily on his memory. (And until he wrote his first novel, *Mary*, about the haunting memory of a Russian first love, VN admitted that the loss of his country and the loss of his Lyussya had remained tightly clasped in his soul.)

Yet as time wore on, the memory of Russia grew more vibrant than Russia herself. Just as people long forgotten reemerge in our dreams, vanished details now beckoned mysteriously through the veil of time. In Germany, he would remember Vyra with a shiver of joy. The smell of white jasmine in bloom, the fey beauty of an autumn day, would call him back to his boyhood. "I am infinitely happy, and so agitated and sad today," he wrote in a letter to his mother in 1921.

Then on certain mornings, it would occur to him that time, in exile too, was taking its insidious toll. When Vladimir visited his mother in Prague, "there was always that initial pang one feels just before time, caught unawares, again dons its familiar mask." Even she was shriveling away.

Long ago, however, Elena Ivanovna had taught him a secret, as though in expectation of imminent loss. She had taught him to observe with the sharpest eye, and remember. And that one endeavor, for both of them, soon cast Vyra in a more radiant halo than it might ever have acquired, had they crossed the border as stowaways, say, in a night train scuttling back to St. Petersburg. "Thus, in a way, I inherited an exquisite simulacrum—the beauty of intangible property, unreal estate—and this proved a splendid training for the endurance of later losses."

There was no turning back. Surviving the revolution, the war, and the anguish of that long Soviet night meant living with a lustrous memory which the present reality of Russia might only extinguish. "What it would be to actually see again my former surroundings, I can hardly imagine . . ." VN, standing in front of his pink granite porch, at 47 Bolshaya Morskaya, looking sullen, one eyebrow lifted higher than the other, in his eyes the puckish light snuffed out. His gaze pale gray, his lips stiff and sallow. (Leningrad, diligently reconstructed after the war, to him no more than a sinister theater set.) And somewhere on the old railing showing off its iron teeth against the sullied pink, by the trees planted just a decade ago, a sign: FOR SALE—COURTESY OF THE DEPARTMENT OF CULTURAL AFFAIRS.

There was no turning back. VN never went back, just as my own father will never go back. "It is another place now," he keeps telling me. But I do know he still dreams,

on nights of heavy sleep, of wind-swept plateaus, wild rasp-
berries, and rides on saddleless horses.


Across the transparent abysses of our lives, we turn our
heads and search for the shores of our past. And since we
can no longer see all too clearly, we imagine new masts and
sails swaying lithely upon the waters. Memory, silently, has
outshined the past, and glistens alone.

## CHAPTER 7

# HAPPINESS, COUNTERCLOCKWISE

(Where the writer dreams up paradise and
the reader leaps straight into it)

*The mirror brims with brightness; a bumblebee has entered the room and bumps against the ceiling. Everything is as it should be, nothing will ever change, nobody will ever die.*

As I again sit at my desk, I realize that, for a while now, I've been ignoring a slight swerving. Like the onset of something; a mild vertigo, not altogether unpleasant.

Terra, I sense, is slowly giving way under my feet. No longer sure of the points on my capricious compass, I wonder about the confines of his territory and mine. Inch by inch, or so it seems, I'm entering stranger waters than I cared to probe when I first started my story. I put down my pen. Shut my eyes. Where was I?

Loss. The cruelty of time. The scandal of pain. The gaping enigma of death. These are the ransoms of consciousness. "The incalculable amount of tenderness contained in the world . . . the fate of this tenderness, which is either crushed, or wasted, or transformed into madness."

And yet. Sidling along this madness, the *possibility* of happiness.

"The first creatures on earth to become aware of time were also the first creatures to smile," he wrote. And the pure starkness of this smile, its "*zaychik*," its "sun blick" (not merely its existence, but its starkness) is, I suspect, the underwater pattern of his world. Perhaps, most exceptionally, of *Ada*. VN's summation on the texture of time, and the nature of happiness.


"We can know the time, we can know a time. We can never know Time," declares Ada. "Our senses are simply not meant to perceive it. It is like——" the tale we are about to be told.

Time does not flow, VN believes. "We feel it as moving only because it is the medium where growth and change take place or where things stop, like stations." But time, regardless, is perfectly still. "Eighty years quickly passed— a matter of changing a slide in a magic lantern." Time passed, and time passing. Speed, like sequence, a delusion.

And perhaps reality is not duration. Tempting though it is to believe it. Amid the coppice of Ardis Park, in the first throes of her infatuation, Ada, sitting next to Van on a bed of moss, exclaims, "But *this* . . . is certain, this is reality, this is pure fact—this forest, this moss, your hand, the ladybird on my leg, this cannot be taken away, can it? (it will, it was). *This* has all come together *here*, no matter how the paths twisted, and fooled each other, and got fouled up, they inevitably met here!'" But *this* was not reality, was it? It twisted and turned *into* reality only in the green-shimmering mirror of memory, the shelter of words.

Memory holds time in cupped hands.

The present is brought forth.

(But "we can never enjoy the *true* Present, which is an instant of zero duration"!)

The present is memory in the making.

(What more is the present?)

Love. Only love. The "flowering of the Present," "the hush of pure memory." A capsule of consciousness.

Or, to be scientifically exact:

$$\frac{\text{LOVE} + \text{MEMORY}}{\text{CONSCIOUSNESS}} = \text{NABOKOVIAN TIME}$$

"Hammock and honey: eighty years later he could still recall with the young pang of the original joy his falling in love with Ada." Eighty years later, Van's happiness would still feed on that first summer. Not with the black claws of melancholy, but with the gleam of lasting presence. "Memory met imagination halfway in the hammock of his boyhood's dawns. At ninety-four he liked retracing that first amorous summer not as a dream he had just had but as a recapitulation of consciousness to sustain him in the small gray hours between shallow sleep and the first pill of the day."

It is in the incident of his falling in love with Ada that Van stumbles upon the true possibility of keeping durational time at bay.

Time folds. Only the present remains.

Van writes in a letter to Demon, his father, a letter which he will never send, "In 1884, during my first summer at Ardis, I seduced your daughter, who was then twelve. Our torrid affair lasted till my return to Riverlane; it was resumed last June, four years later. That happiness has been the greatest event in my life, and I have no regrets."

In his youth, the future was the prospective illusion of a dreamer.

Yet the future does *not* exist, the past is ever present.

("I confess I do not believe in time," whispers VN.)

All that exists is the "glittering 'now' "—the only reality of Time's texture, tingling about us and through us.

Even as he has lost Ada and wanders around the shabby corners of ancient Europe, Van comes to enjoy "the singular little thrill of following dark byways in strange towns, knowing well that he would discover nothing, save filth, and ennui, and discarded 'merry-cans' with 'Billy' labels, and the jungle jingles of exported jazz coming from syphilitic cafés. He often felt that the famed cities, the museums, the ancient torture house and the suspended garden were but places on the map of his own madness." His rivals comically murdered, Ada married off to her ludicrous Arizonian cattle-breeder, and Lucette drowned in her dark-blue night, Van, in perpetual exile, still feels a throb of happiness because the memory of Ardis lingers with him like a palpitating *zaychik*.

One summer alive through a century.

(And as far as this reader is concerned, one moist-lilac morning of giddiness, in a room beyond the looking glass.) The hands of time are clasped.

At present again the world spins. It runs through my fingers. And quietly I cast my net.

"Pure Time, Perceptual Time, Tangible Time, free of content, context and running commentary . . ."

Nothing is forfeited in the radiant *now*.

A firefly pursuing darkness.

A palm resting on a naked shoulder.

A single word making light of gravity.

## CHAPTER 8

# WRITING HAPPINESS: A PRACTICAL HANDBOOK

(Where the writer scribbles ecstatically and
the reader spies over his shoulder)

*E*verything had set out to begin disastrously.

At fifteen, Vladimir had been stirred to compose his first poem when, in the enchanted woods of Vyra, he had observed one drop of rain slide down the vein of a cordate leaf. "Tip, leaf, dip, relief—the instant it all took to happen seemed to me not so much a fraction of time as a fissure in it, a missed heartbeat." The ensuing, heartfelt, poetry was a miserable concoction. And as soon as young Sirin published his first collection, the slim volume fell into the hands of his rabid schoolteacher, a certain Vladimir Hippius, a red-haired poet who, before a roaring class, relished "applying his fiery sarcasm" to the purple stanzas. His teacher's cousin, Zinaïda Hippius, herself a well-known poet, later casually asked Vladimir's father to please tell him that he "would never, never be a writer."

Catapulted into exile, bereft of his boyhood, he persevered.

Overlooking Zinaïda's advice, at twenty-two, he mailed his mother a poem of dubious literary virtues ("Dying nightly, I am glad / to rise again at the appointed hour. / The next day is a dewdrop of paradise / and the day past, a diamond.") In the attached letter, nonetheless, Vladimir added a note that would resonate through the years: "This little poem will prove to you that my mood is as radiant as ever. If I live to be a hundred, my soul will still go round in short trousers." His first, unfinished, novel he tentatively entitled *Schastie, Happiness*. At twenty-five, in "A Letter That Never Reached Russia," he imagined an exiled novelist writing to his lost love, and resolving to speak not of their past but of her lingering presence in his new surroundings. And VN wrote more felicitously than ever before: "The centuries will roll by, and schoolboys will yawn over the history of our upheavals; everything will pass, but my happiness, dear, my happiness will remain, in the moist reflection of a streetlamp, in the cautious bend of stone steps that descend into the canal's black waters, in the smiles of a dancing couple, in everything with which God so generously surrounds human loneliness." A decade later, in Nabokov's most brazenly colorful Russian novel, *The Gift*, Fyodor, his protagonist, contemplates writing "a practical handbook: *How to Be Happy*." A bright filament has been woven.

Style became the illusionist's "baffling mirror."

He spurned the idea that writing could be taught, and to his students at Stanford—the job that would earn him his first American salary—he cautiously advised that the moment an author sets off to write, "the monster of grim commonsense" will "lumber up the steps to whine that the book is not for the general public, that the book will never never—And right then, just before it blurts out the word *s, e, double-l*, false commonsense must be shot dead." In point of fact, VN abhorred "topical trash" (the omnivorous monster), the Literature of Ideas (its self-righteous avatar), and didactic fiction (their duplicitous cousin). He was wary of the tyranny general ideas exert on the general public, for the simple reason that "all 'general ideas' (so easily acquired, so profitably resold) must necessarily remain but worn passports allowing their bearer short cuts from one area of ignorance to another." Great literature, in his eyes, was a feat of language, not ideas. And even then, he did not believe in a grand literary art, only in starkly original artists (such as Shakespeare, Pushkin, Proust, Kafka, Joyce, and himself). So that, in the end, a writer's true biography should amount to no more than the story of his style.

*T*irelessly, he sifted words.

"What the artist perceives is, primarily, the *difference* between things." In VN's glimmering netherworld, literature began with visions. Before fleshing out limbs and torsos with a freshly sharpened pencil, he thought in images, "not in words but in shadows of words." Shadows and shades slowly grading into metaphors. "It was not the sly demon smile of remembered or promised ardor, but the exquisite human glow of happiness and helplessness." These metaphors he regarded as a supple "bamboo bridge," merrily blurring the boundaries of prose and poetry. To think like a poet: *that* was the stamp of his prose style. The scientist (in Vivian Bloodmark's expert opinion) "sees everything that happens in one point of space." Whereas the poet "feels everything that happens in one point of time." And this is how the poet dreams: "A car (New York license plate) passes along the road, a child bangs the screen door of a neighboring porch, an old man yawns in a misty Turkestan orchard, a granule of cinder-gray sand is rolled by the wind on Venus, a Docteur Jacques Hirsch in Grenoble puts on his reading glasses, and trillions of other such trifles occur—all forming an instantaneous and transparent organism of events, of which the poet (sitting in a lawn chair, at Ithaca, N.Y.) is the nucleus."

Ardently he pursued the poet's daydream.

And there lay yet another trick inside his top hat. The event, VN revealed to the attentive ear, does not exist. It must be told. Facts do not exist on their own. They exist because we sketch them into existence. They are true "only in the sense that they are true creatures" of our fancy. The past may only be reconstructed. The prim biographer seeking timelines of truth looks at the world upside down. Composition is the idea. "Splendid insincerity." The literary magicking the literal. The muse of memory dreaming things into events long passed. Language designing figures of time. Did VN truly have a fourteenth-century Tatar ancestor, the very novelesque Nabok Murza? Did he in fact see Kafka on a tram? Did he, one night, meet Véra as she stepped toward him, clad in a black satin mask on a Berlin bridge? (We do not know and do not care.)

Telling countless tales was to him a torture and a pastime.

A torture—because one had to make one's way into the "zoo of words": restive nouns, mottled adjectives, lowing modifiers, braying verbs, the hooves of signs, the crunch of detail, the "wings and claws" of novels. A pastime—because nothing, save perhaps the thrill of butterfly hunting on alpine slopes, could rival in crystalline joy the invention of new worlds. Writers, VN thought, may be Teachers, Storytellers, or Enchanters. The real writer, the Enchanter, is a "fellow who sends planets spinning." To the primeval chaos, he "says 'go!' allowing the world to flicker and to fuse." The Enchanter then recombines atoms, maps his own world, and names the myriad objects it encloses. "Those berries are edible. That speckled creature that bolted across my path might be tamed. That lake between those trees will be called Lake Opal or, more artistically, Dishwater Lake. That mist is a mountain—and that mountain must be conquered." The Enchanter alone can express such general notions as time or space, the color of a sky or the scent of a season, the twitch of a nose or the torment of love, in terms of "unique surprises" which shall then weave the canvas of his style. (And as always when theorizing on aesthetics, Nabokov, mostly, was talking about himself.)

"Invent": one of VN's favorite verbs.

"Fancy is fertile only when it is futile," he said. Creation without cause is the mettle of imaginative writing. Van and Ada's Antiterra, whose breeze blows transparent gusts on VN's style. A style summoning the unseen, seizing light, translating rapture. In a word, Updike once noted, Nabokov writes prose the only way it should be written—that is, E C S T A T I C A L L Y.

Combining stray notes . . .

The texture of his style. The glow of his visual world. A "green rainy day," the "blue snow of notepaper," an "opalescent knee," a "crystal sleep." The surprising poetry of unfamiliar creatures creeping into the tableau: Van's father, Demon, the aging dandy, the raffish rake, turning into a shadowy butterfly, "old Demon, iridescent wings humped, half-rose but sank back again." The injunction of poets and madmen: "Jurors! If my happiness could have talked, it would have filled that genteel hotel with a deafening roar." Their ardent plans of rape and riot. The shiver of sibling consonants: the "failing and fadings" of Van and Ada's summer, "the fatigue of its fugue—the last resort of nature, felicitous alliterations (when flowers and flies mime one another), the coming of a first pause in late August, a first silence in early September." The antiphonal shades: "a state of acute indigestion" caused by eating too many green apples, a servant fired "after letting winds go free" while driving Marina and Mlle Larivière home. All this, and much, much more, amounting to "a steady hum of happiness"—sheer evidence of having lived.

las not everyone *got* his prose style.

When *The Real Life of Sebastian Knight* was published in 1941, the New York Times flatly declared: "All of this might sound nice in another language." Several years later the *New Yorker's* editors tinkered doggedly with "My English Education" and "Portrait of My Mother," which would soon turn into chapters of *Speak, Memory*. Nabokov rejected all edits, stating he preferred "sinuosity, which is my own and which only at first glance may seem awkward or obscure. Why not have the reader re-read a sentence now and then? It won't hurt him." Yet the *New Yorker* hardly renounced its editing frenzy, and VN refuted every query with devilish diligence. Regarding his "Portrait" he wrote back: "There was nobody called 'Joan of Arc.' I prefer, however, her real name, Joaneta Darc. It would be rather silly, for instance, if in a *New Yorker* issue of 2500, I were alluded to as 'Voldemar of Cornell' or 'Nabo of Leningrad.' So, on the whole, I would like to retain 'fatidic accents' and 'Joaneta Darc' if possible." But he had already come across a different sort of misunderstanding. In 1942, on a tour with the lecture "Art and Common Sense," he had just spoken before a women's group when the honorable chairwoman rushed to tell him: "What I loved best was the broken English."

*L*uckily, others found his English quite good indeed.

When the first version of *Speak, Memory*, titled *Conclusive Evidence*, was published in 1951, the critic Morris Bishop wrote his friend Vladimir Nabokov: "Some of your phrases are so good they almost give me an erection—and at my age it is not easy, you know."

*L*ong after he was gone, I went to see for myself.

At the Montreux Palace, on the sixth floor, a liveried woman opened the door to room 65. A thatched roof. A ludicrously small room-with-a-view. On the balcony, two iron chairs and a lanky table staged, presumably, to match the famous photograph of the Nabokovs playing chess. Absolutely everything was new. And Dmitri mentioned, later that morning, that his mother slept in room 63, his father in 64—and that the kitchen was 65. He showed me the text he'd written weeks after his father's death: "That marvelous lectern at which he would begin his writing day is gone. But here, propped against the desk's rear parapet, is the unframed, faded, and dusty reproduction of Fra Beato Angelico's *L'Annunciazione*, brought from Italy by Aunt Elena, with the rigid angel making his announcement on one knee." His father had scrawled beneath the painting a sentence about Gabriel's striking rainbow wings.

*Y*ellow, green, indigo, violet, red.

("All colors made me happy: even gray.") Now I see him. At his desk, taking a peek at his Fra Angelico, lending life to Demon Veen's unfurling "long, black, blue-ocellated" wings. In his eyes lingers a "permanent broad smile." By his writing hand, half-a-dozen white index cards and two pencils. With a third one, he traces his words slowly, distractedly. Skipping from imaginary slide to imaginary slide, studying the exposed film in his mind, he writes out of sequence. He works in the morning, standing up at his lectern, breaks at lunch, continues until dusk, sitting or reclining in a leather armchair by his desk. He seldom writes in the evening. Instead, he watches the sunset with Véra. Or they play chess. At nine, he reads. In summer, he composes stories while butterfly hunting in the hills above Montreux, his inspiration flashing like the yellow wing of a Cloudless Sulphur. In winter, he paces around the glaucous waters of Lake Geneva, plotting extraordinary happiness for his unknown dreamers. A happiness illumined as such in a letter to the editor of *Pale Fire*: "I trust you will plunge into the book as into a blue ice hole, gasp, re-plunge, and then (around p. 126) emerge and sleigh home, metaphorically, feeling the tingling and delightful warmth reach you on the way from my strategically placed bonfires."

. . . . . . . . . . . . . . . .

## CHAPTER 9

# SUNDRY DETAILS
# OF HAPPINESS

(Where the writer showcases his literature and the
reader shows off enlightening commentaries)

**Detail** (n.): the precisely wrought tendrils of a work of art; the secret to discovering pictures concealed within pictures; the sensual spark of the Nabokovian universe.

nce he had crossed over the transparent abyss of exile, borne the loss of his boyhood, his Russian, and his father, VN fervently wrote himself *into* happiness. His writing became the joyous "record of his love affair" with language. A magic carpet on which the lucky reader might zip in and out of a light-infused sky, loll on limpid clouds, ogle at detail after detail of landscapes wild and new.

Because, no matter how snarled the stories, how outlandish the plots, all it amounts to (in the end) is a certain way of looking. Amid spinning planets, where nothing is impossible and mad lovers are immortal, details are the only spell. "Caress the details! The divine details!"

## Detail Sample 1 (*Lolita*)

The LYRICAL, epic, tragic, but never Arcadian American wilds. They are BEAUTIFUL, HEARTRENDINGLY BEAUTIFUL, those wilds, with a quality of WIDE-EYED, UNSUNG, INNOCENT surrender that my lacquered, toy-bright Swiss villages and exhaustively lauded Alps no longer possess. *Innumerable lovers* have clipped and kissed on the trim turf of the old-world mountainsides, on the inner-spring moss, by a handy, hygienic rill, on rustic benches under the initialed oaks, and in so many *cabanes* in so many beech forests. But in the Wilds of America *the open-air lover* will not find it easy to indulge in the most ancient of all crimes and pastimes. POISONOUS PLANTS burn his *sweetheart*'s buttocks, nameless insects sting his; sharp items of the forest floor prick his knees, insects hers; and all around there abides a sustained rustle of POTENTIAL SNAKES—*que dis-je*, of SEMI-EXTINCT DRAGONS!—while the CRABLIKE SEEDS OF FEROCIOUS FLOWERS cling, in a HIDEOUS GREEN CRUST, to gartered black sock and sloppy white sock alike.

I am exaggerating a little. One summer noon, just below timberline, where HEAVEN-HUED BLOSSOMS that I would fain call larkspur crowded all along A PURLY MOUNTAIN BROOK, *we did find, Lolita and I, a secluded romantic spot*, a hundred feet or so above the pass where we had left our car. The slope seemed untrodden. A last PANTING PINE was taking a well-earned breather on the rock it had reached. A marmot whistled at us and withdrew. Beneath the lap-robe I had spread for Lo, dry FLOWERS CREPITATED SOFTLY. *Venus came and went.*

*Humbert Humbert's slyest voice. A moment in the
27,000-mile road trip across America. A stop in the wilds
for a taste of "the most ancient of all crimes and pastimes."
Perhaps one of the more dazzling* Lolita *passages. For
optimal results, read out loud. Words will clip and kiss
in your mouth. Tones will swing and slide like a stream
(elegiac— -and—pastoral—and—faux-pastoral—and—
lecherous—and—droll—and—dark—and—manic—
and—erotic).*

*Next, you may try a pocket-size microscope. Through its
glass, vividly, you'll discover: Words blown up to cartoonish
shapes in toy-bright, hideous green, or heaven-hued color.
A mosaic of details mischievously concealing pictures within
pictures.*

*For a panoramic view, best is to grab a movable telescope.
Through its peephole, from your window perch, you'll glimpse
a reader sprawled in an armchair, legs stretched out on a
hassock. When zooming in, you might also catch a besotted
grin and twinkling brown eyes. Fancy ablaze, forefinger
gliding on the page, it is none other than I, your narrator,
snared in Humbert's maze of images, his crackling love song,
while lace of hem creeps down a Venus thigh. And I've just
uncovered a trove of literary sparklers when . . .*

*SHABANG! Your third-rate springy telescope folds
right back with a snap and hits you in the nose. You
instantly tiptoe away from your window. (And had I not
been so entranced, I might have looked up )*

# DRAWING 1:

## DISCOVER WHAT THE READER HAS SEEN

## Detail Sample 2 (*Ada, or Ardor: A Family Chronicle*)

One afternoon they were climbing the glossy-limbed shattal tree at the bottom of the garden. Mlle Larivière and little Lucette, screened by a caprice of the coppice but just within earshot, were playing grace hoops. One glimpsed now and then, above and through foliage, the skimming hoop passing from one unseen sending stick to another. The first cicada of the season kept trying out its instrument. A silver-and-sable skybab squirrel sat sampling a cone on the back of a bench.

Van, in blue gym suit, having worked his way up to a fork just under his **agile playmate** (who naturally was better acquainted with the tree's intricate map) but not being able to see her face, betokened **mute communication** by **taking her ankle between finger and thumb** as *she* would have a closed butterfly. Her **bare foot slipped**, and the two **panting youngsters tangled ignominiously** among the branches, in a shower of drupes and leaves, **clutching at each other**, and the next moment, as they regained a semblance of balance, his expressionless face and **cropped head** were **between her legs** and a last fruit fell with a thud—the dropped dot of **AN INVERTED EXCLAMATION POINT**. She was wearing his wristwatch and a cotton frock.

("Remember?"

"Yes, of course, I remember: you **kissed** me here, **on the inside**—"

"And you started to strangle me with those **devilish knees** of yours—"

"I was seeking some kind of support.")

*A fall into Eden. A leafy passageway into the enchanted woodlands of Vaniada. The siblings have just met on the country estate of Ardis, and Van is terribly infatuated with pedantic Ada, a truly unusual gamine: naturalist, nifty, and more often than not, naked under her cotton frocks.*

*In this frame, now that you've rubbed your eyes and reassumed your stance with the scope, I may be spotted slinking behind the shrubbery, back slightly arched, two eyes roving through a tangle of twigs. Shamelessly, I'm peering at two children climbing up an apple tree on a summer afternoon. Dead set on trying a hand at VN's own literary diagrams, I pull out a notepad & sharp pencil. My sketch is as follows:* **A.** *is high up in the tree, legs wide open in A-shape.* **V.** *sits right beneath her, arms stretched out in V-shape. Soon, avid* **V.** *seizes ardent* **A.**, *just as their inventor would a frolicking butterfly. The panting youngsters slip. An arrow points downward.* **A.** *falls on* **V.**'s *head, his mouth now on the inside of his sister (in a second he'll "remove a silk thread of larva web from his lip.")*

*An apple falls with a thud* **¡** *(How strangely jumbled my sketch becomes . . . Apples within apple trees within apples . . . ) In this, their mirror world, we blink. Ada and Van are about to experience not sin, but the original ecstasies of incest. A ravenous entrance into beatitude. Their own "Eden National Park" where the luscious apple soon to be devoured, before my-eyes-and-yours, is nothing but themselves.*

# Drawing 2:

# Slice the Luscious Apple

## CHAPTER 10

# APRIL HAPPINESS IN ARIZONA

(Where the writer discovers a dream-bright America and the reader is granted an exclusive interview)

bout ten months after he completed *Ada*, I interviewed VN. We met one late morning of green rain on the shores of Lake Como, where the Nabokovs were summering that year. Following a brisk amble on a path sheltered by profusely fragrant pines, we paced toward a whitewashed cottage overlooking the lake. I'd tentatively requested, in a short, handwritten letter posted to VN the previous month, that he tell me the story of his happiness in America. ("So much of *Ada*," I'd concluded in my awkward hand, "is imbued with the happiness I feel you recaptured in America. Was it this happiness which you then mingled with your fondest memories of northern Russia? And was it America which eventually provided you with a synthesis— a dream-bright territory from which to reinvent Terra?")

Thus was I very much surprised when I noticed VN

*VN and me by Lake Como.*

settling into a wicker chair, a brand-new copy of Dante's
*Inferno* in his hands. "A remarkably literal translation, you
know. As all translations ought to be," he said with an enig-
matic smile, and proceeded to lean over and point to a pas-
sage in Canto One, where the writer encounters Virgil on a
dark and impenetrable forest path. Virgil whispers, "A Poet
was I, and I sang that . . ." As though suspended in time,
nervous even to raise my forehead, I stole a furtive glance
at his dilated pupils. At last, I drew a quick breath, feigned
a cough, opened my red notebook, fidgeted with a felt-tip
pen, looked up, and asked my first question.

There he was, by the raincloud glimmer of that lake,
softly rolling his head-*r* in words like "Russia," while silently

aspiring his middle-*r* in words like "America," "April," and "Arizona."

*If you shut your eyes and think back, what are your instant
   flashes of America?*

[Ever the reluctant speaker, he takes one peek at an index card deftly concealed in Dante, and raises a dreamy eye.] The spasm of a sun-speckled morning in Arizona. All the fragrant afternoons of California. The snow-capped roads of Nevada. The deep-sea blue of a fall sky in Alabama.

*Had you known America before seeing America?*

[He quietly puts the book down.] In Vyra's old park, there was a faraway swamp, of an enchanted blue, which my mother as a child had grown fond of calling "America." In later years, my cousins and I were entertained by the stall-holders, showmen, and jesters of the St. Petersburg fair, whom we called "American inhabitants," and who provided wide-eyed Russian children with Turkish wonders, French hobgoblins, and similar outlandish amusements.

*When you first arrived in America, in May 1940, what did you do?*

Véra, Dmitri and I took a cab to 32 East 61st Street, where our cousin, Nathalie Nabokoff, resided. The meter said "90" and we handed the driver all the money we had in the world, a one-hundred-dollar bill, which he promptly returned. The fare, in fact, was only ninety cents. I am taken to this day with the civility of our first American. (In Russia, the fellow, no doubt, would have left his foreigner penniless.) But when in the spring of 1943 I visited New York again, I leaped out of my cab and pitched the fare on the seat, in the fashion of the brash Romantic hero, which I'd been longing to experience for myself.

*Where were you on D-day?*

A day or two before June 6, 1944, I became dreadfully sick and had to check into a hospital. The din and clatter of the place were driving me mad, and to calm myself I snatched from somewhere a medical dictionary I scanned with glee—for future use in patches and pieces of my American novels. In the end, I ran away, thanks to the careful scheming undertaken by my friend, Mrs. Karpovich, the morning she came to visit me at the ward. I suspect my doctors filed me as potentially lunatic.

*Though you have now moved to Switzerland to live closer to your son, do you consider yourself American?*

As a variant on the apple-pie affair, which I never found appealing, I have coined the more alluring "as American as April in Arizona." Yes, I feel very much at home in America, privately as well as intellectually. I think it one of the most cultured nations in the world, and I have made genuine friends in America, of a kind I was never able to make with natives of Germany or France through all my years there. And it is in America, I should add, that I have found my best readers. So yes, I consider myself an American writer, as writers' passports go, and I still pay American taxes.

*What did America mean to you as a Russian exile?*

In my memoir, I equate the intricate conception of a chess problem with exile, and find the deceptively simple solution to be the final move I had reached through circuitous ways: America! I will not deny it, I have been happier in America than anywhere else in my adult life.

*Did anything in America call you back to the Russia of your youth?*

My butterfly hunting, in a loop of time, seemed at once to resume the butterfly chases of my vanished Vyra. Perhaps because some "fairy wild" regions of northwestern America are surprisingly similar to the Arctic expanse of northern Russia.

*What is your favorite state?*

Please pluralize. Arizona, Nevada, New Mexico, California . . . I am a sun-worshipper, you see. In Wyoming, I com-

posed "The Ballad of Longwood Glen," and it remains to
this day one of my favorite states, and ballads.

*[I glance at my notebook and begin to speak perceptibly faster.]*
*I've been meaning to tell you for years that on a road trip*
*I took across America, the country—Ash Springs, Nevada;*
*Blue Lake, California; Mammoth, Arizona—seemed to me*
*far more "real" as seen through the prism of your* Lolita
*. . .* Lolita, *its landscapes, lakes and Americana, became a*
*lucid slide through which I read the sprawling spaces I was*
*discovering first hand. It lent texture, a lacquer of light, to*
*my own America.*

[He squints and for a second his amber and green eyes narrow to dark almonds.]

*The names of places you dream up have a peculiar quirkiness . . .*

I am fond of my imaginary American names. Elphinstone
and Kasbeam, U.S.A., are two of my favorites. A candy-
cane *concentré* of my America.

*What remained of your "infinitely docile Russian tongue" after*
*you completed your American* Lolita?

*Lolita,* as I have written, was the record of my love affair
with the English language. However, when I tried to
translate my *Lolita* back into Russian, I sensed, alas, that

my marvelous Russian tongue had rusted like a forsaken summerhouse in northern snow. Yet I shall never regret my American metamorphosis. Russian will always be my favorite language. It is my own, and nothing in the realm of linguistic melody can match its dark velvet modulations. But English is a far more supple medium, and I can twist its hot glass at leisure to produce my own translucent beads. Its prose is more delirious, and its plucking precision to my knowledge unparalleled. I have come to believe that one should write, quintessentially, in English.

*What irritates you most about America?*

[He puckers his lips.] The difficulties Americans grapple with in pronouncing unfamiliar names is what irks me most, and I have generally tried to curb American pronunciation as best I could: Vla-DEE-mir I rhymed with redeemer; Na-BOAK-off and Lo-LEE-ta I spelt out in foolproof ways; as to my new novel, I have made my case by adding a phonetically paired subtitle, *Ada, or Ar-dor*, as opposed to *Ada, or Ey-ra*, the little red jaguarundi.

*What do you make of American popular culture?*

With the exception of occasional bad movies and cartoons, I am no personal consumer of popular culture, most of which I consider *"poshlust"* masquerading as real culture. *"POHsh-lust"* is my wonderful Russian word for the trite and vulgar amenities of the philistine way of life. The packaged joy-ride of advertisements—the contented child about to devour his bar of Hershey's chocolate, the airline passenger beaming at the pretty hostess, the pieces of trash pawned off as "powerful" and "stark" novellas. These, nevertheless, I have used in my American novels. So that my *Lolita* is riddled with glossy magazines and gaudy strips, the promised consumer-bliss of U-Beam cottages and Frigid Queens, the clang of jukeboxes, the fizz of cherry sodas. They all form the raw material, the native little tiles of my suburban tableaus.

*Do you enjoy American movies? There are numerous spliced*
  *film reels and noir shots in* Lolita.

I adore American movies! Noirs and comedies, especially. I am often caught laughing uproariously, which appears somewhat contagious.

*Why is your America so exceptionally bright?*

She belongs to my magic palette: her handsome hills and breathless skies, the honest density of her shades have melded so precisely with the horizon of my own imaginary scapes.

*What are some of your most vibrant memories of the New World?*

There are too many. The treasure trove of my New World is boundless. During my years at Cornell, Véra and I drove a hundred fifty thousand miles across North America. She once drove (I have never been able to handle a vehicle) through a blazing storm in Kansas so that we might spot a single butterfly! I remember the alternating rectangles of blue water and green corn unfolding frantically like a fan. The summers at West Wardsboro were delightful. I walked shirtless in the sun. I had not quit smoking yet and my ribs still poke through our faded photographs. Another summer, I was nearly arraigned in New Mexico for dabbing a farmer's tree with sugar and rum—a fabulous sport designed to attract all sorts of interesting moths. On that same trip, in the Grand Canyon National Park, I netted a slender brown beauty, a *Neonympha*, as yet never described. In the mid-1940s, I spent a summer in Utah, an untapped paradise of lepidopteral foray: I would walk a dozen miles a day along mountain ridges, in shorts and tennis shoes, the excitement of chasing butterflies as vivid as that of inventing creatures at my writing desk. In the mid-1950s, Véra and I traveled to Glacier National Park and lived in a one-room cabin . . . These moments outline the sundial of some of my happiest memories.

*What worried you above all in those days?*

In the summers we crisscrossed America, we drove through scores of mountainous regions, swept over in tan dust. By the age of sixteen, Dmitri had become a fearless climber and drove us mad with anxiety. I once wrote to

*Dmitri, conquering his own America.*

him entreating that he relent from putting us through such torture, since we already were a combined hundred and twenty years old.

*When did you first write about America?*

My story "Time and Ebb," which I wrote in the fall of 1944, takes place in America, in a fantasy future. The time is 2024—airplanes are now forbidden and appear mysteriously poetic. As in a rear-mirror, my characters look back to the details of our own era, only to discover that they were pervaded with a tender glow which some-how, in the whirlwind of the present, had escaped their listless notice.

*When did you become a citizen?*

On July 12, 1946, Véra and I became American citizens, and simply reveled in the process. I was struck by the staggering contrast between Russian formality and American flexibility.

*Do you keep any favorite images of your own America?*

I do indeed. Captain Reed's Texan hotel. The slick neon lights of a gasoline station, on the soulless road between Dallas and Ft. Worth, where I managed to catch some fantastic moths . . . These are but two of the countless threads which weave the luminous canvas of my America.

*You claim to be as American as April in Arizona. Have you ever actually seen Arizona?*

Yes, in 1953 I believe, Véra and I headed to Arizona. On an evening stroll, we were assaulted by a rattlesnake, which I expertly killed. On stormy afternoons, I would sit down to write *Lolita*. At nighttime, I read my index cards to Véra, who produced the fair copy.

*And New Mexico?*

I remember an enchanted morning of butterfly hunting in a desert near Santa Fe, where a black mare trailed me for a

mile under the shadowless light. *That* was my America, my
open-eyed, daydreamed, America, where life, once again,
was nowhere but here.

*What did you sense of* Lolita's *impact in America, after it was
published in 1958?*

Contrary to what occurred in France and England, *Lolita*
was not banned in the New World, and America turned
out to be less of a prude than her European cousins. But the
diminutive "Lolita" soon metamorphosed into a panoply
of vulgar avatars—pet names, magazine pinups, spurious
gamines. And I was especially baffled to see a little girl who
appeared to have picked Lolita as her Halloween costume,
all bows and skanties. Other than that, I recall that the citizens of Lolita, a small town in Texas, considered switching
their city's fair name to Jackson.

*What did you feel on traveling back to Europe in November 1960,
nearly twenty years after your arrival in the United States?*

I was an obscure Russian writer when I first sailed to America. On our return journey, our ship, the *Queen Elizabeth*,
had *Lolita* on display, as well as *Laughter in the Dark*, my first
Russian novel translated into English.

*You were later nominated for an Oscar.*

Yes. Stanley Kubrick and James Harris advertised my *Lolita* screenplay, a poetic offshoot of the original, as the finest in Hollywood. And although they did not use it at all, I was indeed, rather absurdly, nominated for an Academy Award. But more to the point: when *Lolita* was selected by Harris-Kubrick Pictures, which bought the film rights, I was reminded of a precognitive dream I'd had in 1916, the year my Uncle Vasily—from whom I'd inherited a fortune that would vanish with the Soviet revolution—had passed away. In this dream, Uncle Vasya had vowed to come back as Harry and Kuvyrkin.

*Will you return to the United States?*

Véra and I long to return to the United States, and several years ago we might have pitched camp in Los Angeles, were it not for Dmitri who had opera engagements in Italy. In Los Angeles, I recall the dashing figure of John Wayne at my first cocktail party, at David O. Selznick's. Sometime later, I met the marvelously pretty Marilyn Monroe. But I had no professional interest in Hollywood as an institution, and I have always been a dreadful speaker and a most disappointing dinner guest. When Miss Monroe asked my wife and me to dinner, we did not attend. Yet to this day I remain enthralled with California for its sun-drenched valleys and stupendous insects. And up until 1964, I avidly dreamed of living in America.

*What about your new novel,* Ada? *With your Antiterra, a twin planet, a magic sort of Amerussia, you have reinvented America . . .*

I have twice at least reinvented America. The America of *Lolita* is as imaginary as the America of *Ada*. But in *Ada*, it is no longer the lawn-green, comely America of my *Lolita*, but an unreal, radiant America steeped into the texture of pure time . . . my metaphor, if you will, for aesthetic bliss.

*Do you miss America?*

I do, but in the blue hills and dells of Switzerland, my wife and I live on as happy as Nabokovs in America.

# NATURAL AND UNNATURAL HAPPINESS

(Where the writer revels in the wizardry of nature and the reader sets out to imitate him)

hen he moved to the Montreux Palace in 1961, VN delighted in the fauna and flora he found along the hills of the Swiss Riviera. He would disappear hours at a time on the heights of Verbier, Crans, and Saas-Fee, to hunt rare creatures which metamorphosed among strawberry shrubs or coniferous boughs. And that—simply that—was happiness.

Nearly half-a-century would pass, as I shall hint at a little later, before I came to consciousness and set out to emulate him. In a nutshell, I myself metamorphosed into an apprentice entomologist (which I can only encourage my readers to emulate in turn.)

# A VERY SHORT HISTORY OF THE BUTTERFLY HUNTER

"When I was younger," VN told a *Sports Illustrated* reporter in Switzerland, "I ate some butterflies in Vermont to see if they were poisonous. I didn't see any difference between a Monarch butterfly and a Viceroy. The taste of both was vile, but I had no ill effects. They tasted like almonds and perhaps a green cheese combination. I ate them raw. I held one in one hot little hand and one in the other. Will you eat some with me tomorrow for breakfast?" Though Nabokov likely never consumed butterflies at breakfast, he was, of course, madly infatuated with the fleeting creatures. Early on, the wonderful glee he derived from butterflies he inherited from his father, who had taught him to distinguish the elegant and arcane choreographies of their habits. The Black Ringlet butterflies which turned up and flaunted their pretty wings only in even years, the Tortoiseshells tightly wrapped in golden chrysalids, the caterpillars of the Blue devouring the larvae of ants, the pulses of Morpho butterflies, with waves of the same, splendid insect emerging all at once, inexplicably, in a cloud of blue dust.

"Summer *soomerki*—the lovely Russian word for dusk. Time: a dim point in the first decade of this unpopular century. Place: latitude 59° north from your equator, longitude 100° east from my writing hand." As a child, VN had fancied himself a future world-class entomologist or, at the very least, an avid curator of Lepidoptera in a vast and marvelous museum. And although he would grow up to write mostly novels, his scientific inquiries led him to discover, name and triumphantly label at least four new species and seven subspecies. His most famous butterfly was the *Lycaeides melissa samuelis* Nabokov, or Karner Blue, of the gossamer wings and shifting tones, celestial blue, but not always. Nabokov declared himself certain that generations of the butterflies he had described as new would soon outnumber the myriad editions of his novels. (In fact, scientific praise, he claimed, meant more to him than anything a literary critic might ever say.) Hence in tribute to his research, more than twelve Blues have now been baptized in Nabokovian overtones, among which are "Lolitas," "Sirins," and "Humberts" (though Lolitas and Humberts remain—scientifically—1,500 miles apart).

For a close-up of entomological glee, to begin with one might imagine VN canvassing the field in his various costumes . . . "as a pretty boy in knickerbockers and sailor cap; as a lanky cosmopolitan expatriate in flannel bags and beret; as a fat hatless old man in shorts." Into his mid-seventies, he could hike for five hours, at times lingering up to three for a butterfly to appear in its familiar habitat. More often than not, passersby and tourists stared at him, puzzled by

"My soul will still go round in short trousers."

his net, mistaking him (or so he later wrote) for a Western Union messenger, or an eccentric vagrant. As such, the protagonist of the Russian *Gift* echoes, perhaps, VN's own experiences: "How many jeers, how many conjectures and questions have I had occasion to hear when, overcoming my embarrassment, I walked through the village with my net! 'Well that's nothing,' said my father, 'you should have seen the faces of the Chinese when I was collecting once on some holy mountain, or the look the progressive schoolmistress in a Volga town gave me when I explained to her what I was doing in that ravine.' " Once, in America, a portly policeman stalked Nabokov for miles, suspicious of an ecstatic old man crisscrossing the countryside alone. Another afternoon, VN was so involved in the quest he accidentally stepped on a bear, but the animal, quite fortunately, was asleep. And although there was nothing ostensibly mystical about the butterfly chases, it was there, in the glades of his hunting adventures, that he found his greatest happiness, and one of its most striking expressions: "The highest enjoyment of timelessness—in a landscape selected at random—is when I stand among rare butterflies and their food plants. This is ecstasy, and behind the ecstasy is something else, which is hard to explain. It is like a momentary vacuum into which rushes all that I love. A sense of oneness with sun and stone. A thrill of gratitude to whom it may concern—to the contrapuntal genius of human fate or to tender ghosts humoring a lucky mortal."

## PROBING THE PECULIAR HAPPINESS OF THE BUTTERFLY HUNTER

For the merry butterfly hunter, nature was, first and fore-most, contained in man himself. In the dark-blue iris of his newborn child, Dmitri, VN saw a "swimming, sloping, elusive something . . . which seemed still to retain the shadows it had absorbed of ancient, fabulous forests where there were more birds than tigers and more fruit than thorns, and where, in some dappled depth, man's mind had been born." In a splendid reflection, thought VN, man's mind, born out of nature, was surely meant to glance right back at its miracle. And he believed, adamantly, that nature would grant the gift of happiness to the careful observer. The gift of netting the primal surprise, the humor, the stunning variations of its tenuous outlines. "Watch," he might whisper, this brown underside of a glistening Blue, that sudden convergence of peacock spots on a wing, the minuscule teeth and spurs of butterfly genitalia . . .

Nabokov's natural philosophy? *First*—OBSERVE! The gardener who omits to set eyes on a turquoise wing has lost a world. *Second*—NAME! The scientist, "without whom the policemen couldn't distinguish a butterfly from an angel or from a bat," will lend a hand. Correctly naming bugs and butterflies is the entryway to basking in the storied detail of their distinctions. Humbert Humbert, for his part, fumbles in viscid ignorance as he gapes at "some gaudy moth or butterfly," "creeping white flies," or "that bug patiently walking up the inside of that window." Van, in comic counterpoint to his obsessive sibling, doesn't take to insects at all. And though he usually keeps his aversion to himself, on an exasperating afternoon, he damns the orange creature (discovered by "Professor Nabonidus") which has captured Ada's amorous attention, an "accursed insect," listlessly settled on an aspen trunk.

In VN's universe, however, the joyousness of pure knowledge serves entirely gratuitous purposes, which is to say— the highest purposes known to man. "I discovered in nature the nonutilitarian delights that I sought in art. Both were a form of magic, both were a game of intricate enchantment and deception." Nature and art may possess the same human measure of bliss. And behind this bliss lies the intuition that the extraordinary designs of art and nature reflect other, more remote and fathomless harmonies. "When one realizes that for all its blunders and boners the inner texture of life is also a matter of inspiration and precision."

TAP! Art in nature! VN was mesmerized by "mimicry," the queerly creative turn of nature which sometimes extends even beyond the rhyme and reason of "natural selection." The formidable ruse of an insect mimicking another to evade a predator, yet taking the art of imitation well past the detection capabilities of its predator. The countless harlequin masks of the natural world. "The enormous moth which in a state of repose assumes the image of a snake looking at you; of a tropical geometrid [moth] colored in perfect imitation of a species of butterfly infinitely removed from it in nature's system . . ." And I am incredibly fond of a shot of VN showing the *Sports Illustrated* reporter, to whom he would later outline his butterfly menu, "disruptive coloration" in the shape of white spots on a wing: "A bird comes and wonders for a second. Is it two bugs? Where is the head? Which side is which? In that split second the butterfly is gone. That second saves that individual and that species." Or here's another shape: "It has a curiously formed letter C. It mimics a chink of light through a dead leaf. Isn't that wonderful? Isn't that humorous?"

TAP! Vice versa in a looking glass, nature in art! From an early story, I recall the eerie, breathless image of "tender, ravishing, almost human happiness" radiating from a nascent moth. In another story, a German collector secretly yearns to explore foreign and tropical butterflies. But just as he is about to set off for Spain, the South Seas and the adventures of a lifetime, he dies of a heart attack on the floor of his own butterfly shop. Though unbeknownst to him, VN writes, the collector had traveled very far indeed, "Most probably he visited Granada and Murcia and Albarracin, and then traveled farther still, to Surinam or Taprobane; and one can hardly doubt that he saw all the glorious bugs he had longed to see—" His imagination as fiercely, as heartrendingly real as "reality." And although it proved far more arduous to picture the tropics, he "experienced still keener pangs when he did, for never would he catch the loftily flapping Brazilian morphos, so ample and radiant that they cast an azure reflection upon one's hand, never come upon those crowds of African butterflies closely stuck like innumerable fancy flags into the rich black mud and rising in a colored cloud when his shadow approached."

TAP strikes the magic wand! Ardors and arbors! Art and nature devising twin wizardry. VN himself, in the guise of a pagan god, creating most of the butterflies in *Ada*—all, perhaps, save one or two. "The song of a Tuscan Firecrest or a Sitka Kinglet in a cemetery cypress; a minty whiff of Summer Savory or Yerba Buena on a coastal slope; the dancing flitter of a Holly Blue or an Echo Azure." He also claimed to have created a tree, though this reader is too wretched a naturalist to pinpoint the suspect. But here is what counted above everything: through hundreds of rippling pages "all was beautiful as neither nature nor art can contrive, beautiful as it only is when these two come together."

# PORTRAIT OF THE NABOKOVIAN AS A WOULD-BE BUTTERFLY HUNTER

Inspired by the happiness of the naturalist, I resolved to try things out on my own.

Truth be told, I grew up in a fairly large city, and my family and I hardly ever made it to the countryside. In my childhood, the closest I came to a cow was at roughly one hundred miles an hour on the highway. From a distance, I had envisioned the animal in milk-bottle guise, covered in creamy curves of black and white bashfully concealing a pink pouch. I was slightly baffled by the hefty grayness of the creature I encountered on the farm-set of a rural inn at the absurd age of seventeen. Needless to say, I bore nearly no interest in animals, and none at all in insects. In sum, I was squeamish. Hawkmoths and caterpillars I found unpleasant at best. Hymenopterans (whom we shall meet again), repellent.

But hunting as I was for Nabokovian bliss, I set out to closely observe, not just moths and butterflies, but a bewildering array of trees and flowers. One rainy afternoon on a hill, I noticed (granted, with a little help) the pungent bristles of wild asparagus, the veinlike patterns of sycamores, the prickly smell of lime trees after spells of rain (etc., etc.). In a surge of irresistible enthusiasm, I soon bought, following hours of perusal in pyramids of manuals, *The Big Book of Flower Gardening: A Guide to Growing Beautiful Annuals, Perennials, Bulbs and Roses*; *Trees of North America: A Guide to Field Identification* (revised and updated); and *Introduction to Butterflies of South America,* Volume 1. I confess to having also stealthily acquired *The Ultimate Butterflies Sticker Book*. I leafed, surveyed, sketched, strove to memorize multitudes of names, before realizing that, alas, I was doing things upside down.

Until at last, unable to stand it any longer, I decided to

experience the thrills of nature in the flesh and promptly
went to acquire my gear. First, I visited a store to purchase
the adequate net for a beginner. Then, I bought a pair of
beige sneakers and camouflage shorts, complete with straw
hat and white cotton shirt. In a canvas satchel, I shoved a
pocket guide and a Band-Aid box to store my catch.

And out I bolted with a butterfly net into a spectacu-
lar national park. A park? *(Que dis-je!)* A paradisal orchard!
In its southern tip, arboreal calico birds were dancing on
arborvitae. Left and right, I saw marigolds, amaranths,
and mulberry groves. As I alertly stepped toward southern
cascades, alders and lime trees saluted with soft rasps and
sweet rustles. Mandrakes and fairy candles paved the paths,
while orioles, crickets, and parakeets congregated by the
jasmine shrubs. Oh, and basilisks, too. What of butterflies,
you wonder? Crowding close to the cascades, I immediately
spotted Blues and Whites frolicking among lupines, spider
plants and melilot. (Foiled!) Sulphurs swung on aspens
while Skippers sat on yellow crocuses. (Foiled again!) Still,
the flicker of American Coppers mingled with the flash
of Red Admirables and the brush of Peacocks while Tiger
Swallowtails vied in splendor with Spring Azures and the
glow of Monarchs and the brightest hues of Nymphalids
fluttering above a spray of offspring.

Overcome by a sense of rapture, keen to partake in
the bounteous delights of nature, I shed my bag and shoes
and socks *et altri*, racing barefoot, skipping among purple
heliotropes and burnberry bushes, net ablaze, light loz-

enges of shade gliding over my naked back. Then at last, I netted my first winged beauty, expertly twitching my wrist to imprison it at once. Swiftly I ran for my bag and extracted the thing from its twirling net. And now to kill it! I grabbed its abdomen, squeezed it nimbly as described in the manual. Curiously, however, I missed by a quarter-of-an-inch, squashing instead a section of its glutinous hind-wing. Nevertheless, minutes later I did manage (all on my own) to accurately match the creature with the drawing of a Cabbage White in my booklet. Ah, the bliss! Netted at last. Sitting quite still in my Band-Aid box.

I am lying a little.

The closest I inched to natural beatitudes were butterflies exhaled by words. In *Ada*, but perhaps especially in *The Gift*. Nature and art joining wiles, that was a language I understood. It was, I knew, the only language susceptible of stirring sentiment, remembrance, when I did venture out and look, from time to time. In *The Gift*, Fyodor recollects the lessons of his father, an illustrious explorer and entomologist: "He told me about the odors of butterflies—musk and vanilla; about the voices of butterflies; about the piercing sound given out by the monstrous caterpillar of a Malayan hawkmoth . . . about the cunning butterfly in the Brazilian forest which imitates the whir of a local bird. He told me about the incredible artistic wit of mimetic disguise." And thus he continued his tale: "Myriads of white Pierids . . . floating further, to settle on trees toward nighttime which stand until morning as if bestrewn

with snow——and then taking off again to continue their
journey——whither? Why? A tale not yet finished by nature
or else forgotten . . . With a strange crazy flight unlike
anything else, the bleached, hardly recognizable butterfly,
choosing a dry glade, 'wheels' in and out of the Leshino firs,
and by the end of the summer, on thistleheads, on asters,
its lovely pink-flushed offspring is already reveling in life.
'Most moving of all,' added my father, 'is that on the first
cold days a reverse phenomenon is observed, the ebb: the
butterfly hastens southward, for the winter, but of course it
perishes before it reaches the warmth.' "

This I did imagine, and pined for unfinished tales and
faraway forests, plotting and dreaming to see them through
the transparency of my own strange flights of fancy.

CHAPTER 12

. . . . . . . . . . . . . . . . . . .

# A READER'S ADVENTURE IN HAPPINESS

(Where the writer retreats to the background
and the reader boldly takes over)

Give me the creative reader;

this is a tale for him.

ou're about to begin the twelfth chapter of *The Enchanter*. Contentedly, you stack two pillows behind your head, curl up in your quilt and switch off the TV. You roll to your side and adjust your lamp. You make sure its halo projects straight onto your page. Reckoning you won't need it, you push your *Oxford English Dictionary* to the far corner of the bedside table. You rub your eyes, yawn with your mouth wide open since no one is there to see, and find yourself spiraling down a cochlea in the dead of night. You look down and dimly distinguish a hole steeped in a golden haze, and with each frantic loop the cochlea appears to vanish overhead. Burning to peer through the haze, you proceed at increasing speed and, all at once, your neck grows extremely thin, your shoulders

incredibly small, your legs are so long you can barely feel your feet, and whiz—you slip into the hole.

After a dreadfully long fall, you land, spread-eagled, in a larch wood. Dazed, you slowly get up, dust off your pajamas, and glance around. About two yards to your left, you spot a red chessboard and three wooden signposts, with destinations scrawled in white chalk: DODO'S LAIR, DANDELION DEN, DEMONIA. A brook runs parallel to the third sign, and though it seems slightly out of season in this breezy spring, you catch sight of a Lysandra butterfly dipping its slender snout in a countercurrent. As soon as you draw near, it disappears. And for a second, instead of the quivering insect, you see your own image, squarely staring back at you. Startled by your own expression, you take a step back and wonder.

You have read in a chronicle that certain bewitched travelers who've made their way to Demonia never returned. Besides, since ancient times, "emperors, dictators, priests, puritans, philistines, political moralists, policemen, postmasters, and prigs" have warned that Demonia is a hazardous region, where inexperienced travelers suffer severe delusions. Demonia, they whisper, lies beyond the highest mountains, in a sand-swept land encircled by white birds of prey and dappled insects . . . You are somewhat hesitant, but you tell yourself that, as the great Vivian Darkbloom once noted, "curiosity is insubordination in its purest form," and with a shiver of trepidation you embark on the third road.

Soon, you reach the edge of the larch wood and amble

past a pallid lake and a barren of pines. A few stretches later, you hit upon a narrow mountain pass. And as you are trudging uphill, panting and flushed, you start humming a little nursery tune in the morning air:

*Ever drifting down the stream—*
*Lingering in the golden gleam—*
*Life, what is it but a dream?*

Hours later, it seems, you chance upon a bright new sign pointing upward: NOTCH OF UNKNOWN DREAM-ERS. This time, there is only one sign, so you calmly walk along. After hiking far more than you had anticipated, you are about to sit on a boulder when you notice a book a visitor must have left behind. With a slight jolt, you contemplate whether he might never have made the journey back, since the book—*Ada, or Ardor: A Family Chronicle,* by Vladimir Nabokov—is still lying there, untouched. You crack it open on the wrong end, a bad habit you are secretly embarrassed about, and you take a peek at the last pages:

*Ardis Hall—the Ardors and Arbors of Ardis—this is the leitmotiv rippling through* Ada, *an ample and delightful chronicle, whose principal part is staged in a dream-bright America—for are not our childhood memories comparable to Vineland-borne caravelles, indolently encircled by the white birds of dream?*

Though you know you really mustn't, you quickly skim
over the bottom paragraph:

*The rest of Van's story turns frankly and colorfully upon his
long love-affair with Ada. It is interrupted by her marriage to
an Arizonian cattle-breeder whose fabulous ancestor discovered
our country. After her husband's death our lovers are reunited.*

You're a bit puzzled. You open the book again and, on
the first page, examine the family tree which ushers in the
chronicle. Eponymous Ada marries one Andrey Vinelander
(the cattle-breeder). You scratch your nape and flip back
again to the end of the book. "Dream-bright" . . . you like
that expression and already plan on using it somewhere,
discreetly passing it off as your own. In fact, you like the
entire sentence, you like the unctuous sensation of its combined words, you can feel it sifting through you like a caravelle gliding in green-blue waters. Though, come to think
of it, you're not exactly sure what it means. "For are not our
childhood memories comparable to Vineland-borne caravelles, indolently encircled by the white birds of dream?"
You are irritated, but increasingly curious. "Borne," past
participle ("bear, bore, borne," murmurs an Oread in your
ear). "Caravelle" retrieves straight away, from a grade school
history book, the drawing of the handsome vessel, all masts
and sails, which brought Columbus over to the New World.
As to "vineland," lowercase *v*, you suspect it simply means
a land of vines. But how you wish you had that dictionary

handy to verify . . . So you look around, half hoping you might find one lying somewhere in the weeds, or at least a book of rules for understanding obscure sentences, when, for a split second, you could swear a demonic little creature, crouched behind a thorny bush, green iris and fox-red hair, is gazing brashly at you. She spurts a mermaid's laughter, and before you've had time to breathe, she runs away in the wind, weightless skirt floating in midair. A moment later you notice a brand-new *Oxford English Dictionary* (which definitely wasn't there before, you think to yourself) neatly positioned by the shrub. On the cover of the large volume is a paper label with the words "READ ME" carefully inscribed in capital letters. Though fairly bewildered, you slowly reach out and leaf through the volume until you've found "vineland": "a land particularly suited to the growing of vines." What then is a "Vineland-borne caravelle"? A caravelle bearing vines? A vineland bearing a caravelle? A caravelle made of vine wood? In doubt, you look up "caravelle," "(kār'ə-vĕl') n. Nautical. Any of several types of small, light sailing ships, especially one with two or three masts and lateen sails used by the Spanish and Portuguese in the 15th and 16th centuries." You being you, the word "lateen" nettles you, so you look that one up, too: "a triangular fore-and-aft sail used especially in the Mediterranean."

Now stuck in a nautical dream, you pace back and forth along the ledge. And for an instant, you can almost surely discern an elfin silhouette whisking toward timberline. Then out of the blue, it hits you. You remember the last time you boarded an airplane (it seems like centuries ago today). You remember the voice of the skipperess in her monotonous lilt: "After we are airborne, passengers are kindly required to wait for the signal before unfastening their seatbelts." Airborne, airborne, Vineland-borne . . . Could it simply mean toward the vineland? But what vineland? And what childhood memories glide toward vineland in bird-encircled caravelles? You check "vineland" once again, and this time you mark a second definition you'd only glossed your eyes over the first time. "Vineland" (uppercase *v*): "A city in S New Jersey." Could our caravelle be dutifully plying the waters from Spain to south New Jersey? Thankfully, sandwiched between the pages of your hefty dictionary is a roadmap of the United States (and though on a regular day you might have been stumped, at present it appears quite natural). You pull it out and scan it in the afternoon light, the sunrays stroking the curves of reds and yellows. And you find it. Vineland, well to the west of New Jersey's coastline, at least thirty or fifty miles. You consider for a desperate but earnest minute whether Vineland might be famous for its caravelle warehouses, then you give up, admitting (a bit grudgingly) that you have reached a dead-end. In a last-ditch effort, you pull out of your pajama pocket a tattered *Guidebook to Field Trips in North America* and begin to leaf through the index . . . down, up, down, up, Vista Palace, Vineyards of California, Vineland, CANADA! You turn back the pages and utter a chesty **HA!** eerily resounding against the jagged cliffs: "Legend has it that one

thousand years ago an ancient Viking Leif the Lucky discovered a pleasant, warm and fertile land west of Greenland.
He called it Vineland. In the spirit of Viking adventure and
discovery, Vineland would like to help you discover the
natural splendor and tranquility of ancient Vineland, filled
with warm, modern maritime hospitality." Vineland, Vineland . . . Vinelander "whose fabulous ancestor discovered
our country"! You get up and gambol round your boulder.
"For are not our childhood memories comparable to . . ."
white lateens swiftly sailing toward the New World like
young, languorous dreams of a future in the making.

You pluck up your courage and walk on toward the
purple summit you clearly make out in the distance. The
sun has begun to set in the foothills and draws a crimson
veil over the far-off plains. But before you can pause to take
breath and quietly survey the new surroundings, the book
you have snatched from its boulder slips from your hands
and opens to the same, dream-bright page as before (which
you must have pressed hard the first time around). You lift
it up to your eyes and in the waning light you read: "Before
we can pause to take breath and quietly survey the new
surroundings into which the writer's magic carpet has, as it
were, spilled us . . ." You are not surprised. You expected
something like this would happen, or at least you hoped
it would. You are being impertinently dreamed by your
book. You flip back to page 1.

## CHAPTER 13

# THE CRUNCH
# OF HAPPINESS

(Where the writer uses scintillating words

and the reader swallows them one at a time)

here are certain words that dazzle and delight, scintillate and sparkle like stars on a see-through night, luminaries of luminescence that lure the eye toward fiery orbs thus far unseen. Here are a few passing shimmers which shine toward me like gold-dust on illumined manuscripts. Although for some, these may remain dormant—mere letters indolently ignoring one another—perhaps they will, as you doze off a little, graciously join hands and gleam in your palpebral night. And perhaps sundry other letters will tumble before your eyes and taunt you with their tunes, while my foolishness skips past them completely. But these are the ones which kindle my curiosity. A crunch of luscious literary glee.

"READ ME"

# AZURE-BARRED

"Fabulous, insane, exertions that left me limp and azure-barred." (*Lolita*)
Zany bands of blue haze floating about the cerebellum.

# BLISS

"I realized that the world does not represent a struggle at all, or a predaceous sequence of chance events, but shimmering bliss, beneficent trepidation, a gift bestowed on us and unappreciated." ("Beneficence," *Stories*)
A Batch of Lucid Images Sliding over Sibilants. Also, the thrill of seeing dark nebulae slowly turning into luciferous spheres.

# COCHLEA

"For a while he lay on the black divan, but that seemed only to increase the pressure of passionate obsession. He decided to return to the upper floor by the cochlea." (*Ada*)
A fairytale stairway lifted and instantly slipped into Chapter 12.

# CONCOLOROUS

"When I first met Tamara—to give her a name concolorous with her real one—she was fifteen, and I was a year older.

The place was the rugged but comely country (black fir, white birch, peatbogs, hayfields, and barrens) just south of St. Petersburg." (*Speak, Memory*)

A con–binational Latinate adjective. *"Tamara et Lyussya puellae concolorae erant. Catamounti, cougari, pantheri et pumae felini concolori sunt."*

# FATA MORGANA

"The town was newly built, or rebuilt, on the flat floor of a seven-thousand-foot-high valley; it would soon bore Lo, I hoped, and we would spin on to California, to the Mexican border, to mythical bays, saguaro deserts, fata morganas." (*Lolita*)

Melting mirages or ethereal sorceresses. At high noon, one may hear Morgan fairies sing that love—the true love of odes and sonnets, erotic confessions and ardent chronicles— is born on blessed mornings when whimsical knights gallop toward faraway moats, crenulated towers and creaking doors. And once they hear a maiden's fluty voice . . . (For the various outcomes of this tale, please flip back to Chapter 5).

# FRITILLARY

"And the savor of the grass stalk I was chewing mingled with the cuckoo's note and the fritillary's take-off." (*Speak, Memory*)

A brown butterfly—of the charming Nymphalidae

family—sporting black spots on its forewings and silver spots on the underside of its hind wings. May trigger interesting flashes of synesthesia pertaining to the fricative delights of fluttering fritillaries, or the flights of fancy mingling frosted *millefeuilles* and mottled wings.

## GLOAMING

"A large, alabaster-based kerosene lamp is steered into the gloaming. Gently it floats and comes down; the hand of memory, now in a footman's white glove, places it in the center of a round table." (*Speak, Memory*)
A word or creature gently floating in the dusk. A second before sunset, the darkening wings of a Luna moth about to settle on a hickory.

## HEAVENLOGGED

"A very light cloud was opening its arms and moving toward a slightly more substantial one belonging to another, more sluggish, heavenlogged system." (*Lolita*)
Gorged with sun-clouds. Also, the abdomen after-bliss of azure-barred nights.

## HYMENOPTEROID

"Consider the tricks of an acrobatic caterpillar (of the Lobster Moth) which in infancy looks like bird's dung, but after molting develops scrabbly hymenopteroid appendages and baroque characteristics, allowing the extraordinary fellow to play two parts at once." (*Speak, Memory*)

Sophisticated-sounding though unpleasant creatures engaged in metamorphosis (excluding butterflies). Liable to sting or pierce. Will leave a lasting impression if used *offhandedly* in refined dinner conversation to recount the unfortunate collateral damage of a subtropical vacation.

## HYPERBOREAN

"It was also a particularly severe winter, producing as much snow as Mademoiselle might have expected to find in the hyperborean gloom of remote Muscovy." (*Speak, Memory*)

The dim and glacial winter of northern Russia as romanticized by a French governess arriving by train in St. Petersburg. The Hyperboreans may be seen drifting like phantoms over glazed-blue ice beyond the north wind, at the mythical confines of Mother Muscovy.

## KZSPYGV

"The word for rainbow, a primary, but decidedly muddy, rainbow, is in my private language the hardly pronounceable: *kzspygv*." (*Speak, Memory*)

A sun-flooded hieroglyph. In a single breath: "huckleberry k" "thundercloud z" "azure and mother-of-pearl s" "unripe

apple p" "bright-golden y" "rich rubbery g" "Rose Quartz
v"—*kzspygv*.

# LAMBENCY

"I had nothing—except one token light in the potentially
refulgent chandelier of Mademoiselle's bedroom, whose
door, by our family doctor's decree (I salute you, Dr Sokolov!), remained slightly ajar. Its vertical line of lambency
(which a child's tears could transform into dazzling rays of
compassion) was something I could cling to, since in absolute darkness my head would swim and my mind melt in a
travesty of the death struggle." (*Speak, Memory*)
The L-shaped Lines of Light you shall soon spot beneath an
obscure door.

# LOAM

"As I focused my eyes upon a kidney-shaped flower bed
(and noted one pink petal lying on the loam and a small
ant investigating its decayed edge) or considered the tanned
midriff of a birch trunk where some hoodlum had stripped
it of its papery, pepper-and-salt bark, I really believed . . ."
(*Speak, Memory*)
Poetic compost. Harks back to lines of verse by a gifted
poet: "In the gloaming I roam / through fulvous foams of
loam."

# NYMPHETLAND

"My Lolita . . . smelling of orchards in nymphetland; awkward and fey, and dimly depraved, the lower buttons of her shirt unfastened." (*Lolita*)
A wonderland as seen through field glasses atop an apple tree in Humberland.

# PALPEBRAL

"The colored spot, the stab of an afterimage, with which the lamp one had just turned off wounds the palpebral night." (*Speak, Memory*)
A chic synonym for the dark underworld beneath closed eyes. The black screen lazily unrolling before one dozes off, book in hand.

# PERIS

"Demon's senses must have been influenced by a queer sort of incestuous (whatever the term means) pleasure . . . when he fondled, and savored, and delicately parted and defiled, in unmentionable but fascinating ways, flesh (*une chair*) that was both that of his wife and that of his mistress, the blended and brightened charms of twin peris, an Aquamarina both single and double, an orgy of epithelial alliteration." (*Ada, or Ardor*)

A beguiling fairy of Persian mythology. A beauty fallen from paradise, or in a turquoise-framed mirror, a female demon. A clue if you flip back to Chapter 2.


# PURL

"When that pearly language of hers purled and scintillated."
(*Speak, Memory*)
To undulate and murmur like a streamlet of French words.
"*Désirez-vous une tartine au miel?*" (The lips should form a tiny *o*.)


# ROSE QUARTZ

"Today I have at last perfectly matched *v* with 'Rose Quartz' in Maerz and Paul's *Dictionary of Color*." (*Speak, Memory*)
The color of Voldream Manor, property of Voldemar the Magician (also alluded to as "Voldemar of Cornell" in Chapter 8.) In his rose-quartz attic, Voldemar stored a colossal dictionary, containing such rich and strange formulae as were utilized only by himself. On a scorching afternoon in late August, however, Voldemar at last summoned his nosy apprentice and pointed to a crystal ladder leading all the way up to the roof. The apprentice, who needn't be asked twice, raced up the ladder, hit the rose-quartz ceiling with a dull sound of his egg-shaped cranium, and zealously leaned over Voldemar's book of books. Somewhere,

so very far away it seemed, Voldemar was yelling something about drives or droves. The apprentice, oblivious to
the voice which had now dwindled to a faint whisper, was
already flipping through the book at furious pace. But *just*
as he was deciphering his first definition, he caught sight of
himself—as though on a Miramax movie screen—racing
madly in the midst of a rocky plain, somewhere in a distant century, toward galloping Tatars armed with spiky and
awesome weapons . . .

# SCIMITAR

"Its tremendous desk with nothing upon its waste of dark
leather but a huge curved paper knife, a veritable scimitar
of yellow ivory carved from a mammoth's tusk." (*Speak,
Memory*)
One might fancy this stylish scimitar as Nabok Murza's
weapon of predilection. The mammoth-blade which Nabok
held close at hand to taunt Teutonic bellies darting toward
Tatary. (You may flip back to Chapter 8 for a cameo.)

# STRATAGEM

"The interest that perfect strangers showed in regard to
him seemed alive with dark stratagems and incalculable
dangers (beautiful word, stratagem—a treasure in a cave)."
(*Nikolaï Gogol*)
Calls forth strategically hidden treasures of other caves:

bearcat—a large feline; isinglass—a bee frozen in crystal; zooglea—a happy experience in a cage.

## SUB ROSA

"He had beautiful manners, a sweet temper, an unforgettable handwriting, all thorns and bristles (the like of which I have seen only in the letters from madmen, that, alas, I sometimes receive since the year of grace 1958), and an unlimited fund of obscene stories (which he fed me sub rosa in a dreamy, velvety voice, without using one gross expression)." (*Speak, Memory*)
A secret rose culled from a famed medieval rhyme (customarily accented on the *ultima*): "*Sub rosa a wily poet shall net / his alluring peris in a sonnet.*"

## UMBELLIFER

"The Swallowtail of June 1906 was still in the larval stage on a roadside umbellifer." (*Speak, Memory*)
A succulent plantlet of the parsley family. Or its cavernous echoes: umbrella birds, umber umbels, umbelliferous umbellules, Umbriel umbras, umbilicate umbrellas.

## UVULA

"Hysterical little nymphs might, I knew, run up all kinds of temperature—even exceeding a fatal count. And I would have given her a sip of hot spiced wine, and two aspirins, and kissed the fever away, if, upon an examination of her lovely uvula, one of the gems of her body, I had not seen that it was a burning red." (*Lolita*)

A V-shaped ruby mimicking its A-shaped sibling in sensual symmetry.

## CHAPTER 14

# HAPPINESS THROUGH THE LOOKING GLASS

(Where the writer peers beyond the limits of
life and the reader steals a furtive glance)

s he is about to divulge a secret, "the veRRy essence of things," I visualize VN standing on his toes behind a lectern, his mouth opening in slow motion, uvula about to quiver in its crimson cave. "I know more than I can express in words, and the little I can express would not have been expressed, had I not known more."

His secret is to be captured (net in hand, tiptoeing stealthily) behind his words, in the nether side of his prose. His blueprint of happiness.

It starts with an observation. It ends, possibly, with a creative kind of madness. And I suspect our writer amplifies his own penchant when he describes a certain "lunatic who constantly felt that all the parts of a landscape and movements of inanimate objects were a complex code of allusion to his own being, so that the whole universe seemed to be conversing about him by means of signs." Life entire a maze of signs, faint dots of light drafting designs as yet unknown.

VN's stories abound in sequences of identical figures, twinned dreams, repeat occurrences. They come in the guise of enchanted room numbers, receding galleries of mirrors, or invented butterflies (the list could extend into an infinitely curving sentence). "Some law of logic should fix the number of coincidences, in a given domain, after which they cease to be coincidences, and form, instead, the living organism of a new truth," Van muses, as though responding in a far-off corner of time to Humbert, who in his own story keenly records "those dazzling coincidences that logicians loathe and poets love."

For such is the exhortation of poets: *"Open your own eyes and survey until you see!"* Until the dazzling coincidences, at once, clear as day, reveal the lining of a new truth, a splendid pattern, a glint of significance. To observant men, these Nabokovian patterns, magically, will offer the inkling of an "otherworld," the ineffable beauty and concord of which is cause for infinite happiness. "I know more than I can express in words—" Folded deep into the texture of his fiction, there is, ultimately, a faith in the extraordinary light tingling above, beneath, through, and around us.

"Not text, but texture . . . Not flimsy nonsense, but a

web of sense," says the poet in *Pale Fire*. "Yes! It sufficed that I in life could find some kind of link-and-bobolink, some kind of correlated pattern in the game."

Then, it is only up to us to discover that the weave of verse is the very fabric of our own lives.

. . . . . . . . . . . . . . . . . . . . . . . . . . . . . . . . . . . . . . . . . . . . . . . . . . . . . . . . . . . . . . . . . . .

A pessimist and, like all pessimists, a
ridiculously unobservant man . . .

. . . . . . . . . . . . . . . . . . . . . . . . . . . . . . . . . . . . . . . . . . . . . . . . . . . . . . . . . . . . . . . . . . .

Seeing, ceaselessly seeing; gleaning consciousness. Then attempting, at every turn, to record and recombine its elements. At core, the gift of the Nabokovian novel is this, just this: a call to whom-it-may-concern to capture photon after photon of fleeting life.

And in all these years, I have derived such glee from madly recombining, that—as VN once told Edmund Wilson of spreading trees with rum for nights of mothing—I am tempted to say, "Try, Bunny, it is the noblest sport in the world."

It's as much a matter of remembering and connecting, as it is of inventing, at times. Thus from composites, I recomposed. From elements of VN's true story, I imagined other stories, new beginnings. And when some form of meaning, likely half-invented (but all the more relevant) emerged, that was glee, a sense of harmony, of "oneness with sun and stone." I will not bore you with the detail of my obsessions. Suffice it to say that now and again, as Humbert salutes his

"Dream Blue" automobile at the end of *Lolita* ("Hi, Melmoth, thanks a lot, old fellow"), I secretly saluted VN. That butterflies, inevitably, invaded my field of vision, orange, brown, blue insects, shimmering in the margins of the most indiscriminate stuff (mulberry bushes, water bottles, bikinis). That the number 23 (April 23, VN and Shakespeare's joint birthdays) turned up everywhere, bills, dates, hours, minutes, flight numbers (2304, Paris to Geneva; flunky with blue butterfly sticker awaiting on arrival), digits proffered casually by life's flashing dial. That the invented tree I could not find for Chapter 11, I came across on opening *Ada* at random the very night I finished the chapter ("sealyham cedar" is the culprit, I believe). That after I considered naming the last section of this book "On one thousand shades of light," I stepped outside and glanced at a shop window and noticed a ragged book titled *One Thousand Lights*. That when I read about VN's Fra Angelico print, mentioned in Chapter 8, I realized I had three different versions of that same angel kneeling over my own desk in New York. That just as I switched on my American television for the first time in months, the second word I heard was Nabokov (and this was cable news!). That a day or two after reading about a six-inch-long caterpillar with "fox-furred segments" (which I'd instantly associated with the green and copper shades of Lucette), I detected a hideous little worm, rusty-furred with spikes of green floss, slothfully tramping along the inner edge of my bathtub . . . Slowly, ridiculously, I imagined—yes, imagined, nothing but that—my life stippled with "one of those repetitions, one of those thematic 'voices' with which, according to all the rules of harmony, destiny enriches the life of observant men."

Then there was Dmitri, whom I had met in the winter of 2003. At his home in Montreux, during one of my visits in the following years, I had listened to a crackling tape of his basso performance in *Boris Godunov*. I had listened to the frenetic tale of his life, mountaineering in Wyoming and British Columbia, singing engagements in Medellín and Milan, racing fast cars and off-shore boats, rejoicing, it seemed, in every gap left by VN's biography, before devoting these last decades of his life to feverish translations of his father's works, from Russian to English and Italian.

I had listened to him speak of his own tribulations with *Lolita*, a journalist quipping he was "Lolito," only son of *Lolita*'s creator; lewd women assuming lewder idiocies about his father's life. I had looked for hours at his library, spotting stylized book covers I had never seen; versions of his father's novels in Hungarian, Turkish, or Arabic; rows of archived documentaries; Russian photographs of the Nabokov grandparents. I had scrutinized the 1960s shots of VN and Véra, the sepia sunshine that continued to glisten in their eyes. I remember, in particular, one evening in wintertime when I stood for hours before narrow bookshelves, skimming through VN's own books: *Macbeth*, a volume on the history of Western painting, another on

French Romantic poetry. I read his handwritten commentaries in the margins, *"splendid," "wrong!!!"* Silently, I had the absurd feeling of crossing life threads with Dmitri, a droll sense of wonder at discerning a contrapuntal theme to my four-hundred-mile missed encounter with his father. I looked at Dmitri's clear blue gaze, tuned in to the grain of his voice, so close to his father's as one may catch it in recordings, and distinctly heard the manner both Nabokovs pronounce their soft, White-Russian *t*'s. And I recalled the "thrill and glamour" that a young expatriate "finds in the most ordinary pleasures as well as in the seemingly meaningless adventures" of a life. In short, I was happy.

A few months later, in the spring of that same year, as I stood by a gloomy store window to hide from a pelting, quasi-tropical rainstorm in New York, I overheard a Russian couple chattering briskly on my right. Having myself plodded through long and miserable years of intensive Russian ("liquid verbs in *ahla* and in *ili*"), I strained to decipher sentences here and there when, moving slightly to see their faces, I could not fail to identify a ruby-and-diamond incrusted butterfly, outrageously large, in the window behind me. (These grating butterflies, I thought.) Then, turning back to the street side, I looked up and read through the slits of moist lashes the green sign, marked in slim New York City white font: Dimitrios Pathway. Calmly, I smiled and disappeared into the rain.

A pessimist and, like all pessimists, a
ridiculously unobservant man . . .

On certain days, desperately do we call on signs to salute us, to hint even lightly at what we desire them to say. We might make wild amends to the dead we've never loved, and like Van wish for a sign, "an unequivocal, and indeed all-deciding, sign of continued being behind the veil of time, beyond the flesh of space." But of course nothing comes in response, not a petal, not a gnat.

And yet, every so often, if we dare imagine they might, signs will swiftly flicker across the darkness. We may immediately make up their whimsical meanings, or read them into the fabric once we eye them from afar.

They speak in a whisper, a draft of phrases, like an arcane language almost out of earshot. "We are not going anywhere," VN insists, "we are sitting at home. The other world surrounds us always and is not at all the end of some pilgrimage. In our earthly house, windows are replaced by mirrors; the door, until a given time, is closed; but air comes in through the cracks." A sough, a stifled intonation, a song forgotten yet eerily familiar. And right there, in that "glassy darkness," emerges "the strangeness of life, the strangeness of its magic, as if a corner of it had been turned back for an instant," so that we may glimpse "its unusual lining." Or sense, like the protagonist of *The Gift*, that "all this skein of random thoughts, like everything else as well—the seams and sleaziness of the spring day, the ruffle of the air, the coarse, variously intercrossing threads of confused sounds—was but the reverse side of a magnificent fabric."

Literature is but scintillating texture. " 'Iceling' or 'inglice.' I think that *some day* that will happen to the whole of life," writes Fyodor in *The Gift*. The demonic artistry of words perhaps conceals "galaxies divine," where death might be no more than a lifted corner of the eternal present.

Broad daylight. The waking hour. A dream no longer, for it is "certainly not then—not in dreams—but when one is wide awake, at moments of robust joy and achievement, on the highest terrace of consciousness, that mortality has a chance to peer beyond its own limits, from the mast, from the past and its castle-tower. And although nothing much can be seen through the mist, there is somehow the blissful feeling that one is looking in the right direction."

Now imagine this trail of light.

*Wide awake.*

## CHAPTER 15

# PARTICLES OF HAPPINESS

(Where the writer uncovers one thousand shades of light and the reader encounters him again)

Light (n.): The medium of choice for netting
the marvel of being-in-the-world.

 ne night in early March, I had a see-through vision of *sun-spangled* water parted by a *mesh of sunshine*. When I woke up, the slats of a Venetian blind had already striped two feet lazily breaching out of my twin bed. *Icicles gloriously burned in the low sun*, and I watched the droplets of water trickling down behind the slats while the *sun broke into geometrical gems*. I pulled up the blinds and admired the first *sea of sunshot greenery* I had seen since the last days of my slow summer. The sky above formed a *lucid, turquoise space* that the receding cold ruffled with the first *brilliant convulsions* of spring. An *unusual euphoria of lightness* had set in. I rushed downstairs and stepped with naked soles on the freezing, *sun-mottled* bricks, shut my eyes and slipped under a pellucid dream. Beneath its soft surface, I felt the *red sun of desire and decision* burning like *roundlets of live light*. But

when I opened my eyes, something appeared to have changed in the interval. Perhaps it was the *brilliant veil* which had covered the surrounding hills, or the *apple-green light* behind the miniature house crouched near the garden gate, or else the *lurid gleam* that emanated from the garage.

Within seconds, the sky darkened and poplars floated in a *dusk-mellowed* light. A blackbird sang a quavering trill, and *sealskin-lined scarlet skies* threatened the last *beaming vestige of sunlight.* I tiptoed toward the garage, spellbound by a *handful of fabulous lights* beckoning in the distance. Tentatively, I stepped over the lawn *under the pale star-dusted firmament.* And all at once it was summer. A *radiant night, satiated with moonlight,* as bright as an *iridescent Persian poem.*

The *moth-flaked porchlight* exuded a warm haze. A lonely glowworm writhed around a stone slab. Fireflies flickered and vanished like *golden ghouls or the passing fancies of the garden.* The garage door looked farther and farther away from the *arabesques of lighted windows* shining against the flow of night. Through a *trick of harlequin light,* the road shimmered ahead, and the slabs burned in the lawn. For a moment, it seemed as though someone had laid out *magical lumps of calcium carbide* knowingly pointing the way to the garage door. The glass panes over the doors radiated with a *selenian glow.* Then *light collapsed.*

I approached him. He was writing neatly on a small white card propped up on a shoebox. I noticed the *sudden radiance of a lone lamp.* By his foot lay an *emerald lantern.* And in that *arena of radiance,* he peered at me over his glasses, which had acquired the *translucent green tone of grapes.* He smiled like a sphinx (was it the *bright leer of madness?*). "Ah, here you are. I have been waiting for you. I thought you might not come." His *pallor shone*, his *blackness blazed* in the *scaly light.* I opened my mouth and said nothing, gaping instead at the *tender, moist gleam* in his lower eyelid. "Well, child, now that you are here, you might as well sit down." He ran a painter's eye on my naked feet, "You're quite small. What do you need?" My eyes round as crystal balls, I uttered two words, "My book . . ." "Yes, I know." "I'd like to ask . . . ," I began, invisible bubbles forming soundless shapes on my lips. A *double gleam*, a perfect L, glided beneath the garage door. "A *limpid and luminous letter.* The prismatic Babel of hap——" he whispered and disappeared. And I thought I heard one last word, "Yclept!"

Mystified, I stepped out, drawn by the *Lebanese blue* of the sky. Far, very far away, through diffuse *layers of light*, I made out the silhouette of a man walking toward the horizon with his *emerald lantern*, before dissolving into the morning air like a *violet-tinged nimbus of gaslight. A small luminous beetle* scurried past my ankles. I sat down, captivated by the sky, spying a *limpid dawn*, surveying the *dappled sun* and the *pale-lemon light* of a new morning. I stared at *glades of lucid smoothness.* Soon the day *sparkled from end to end.* And in a *gleam of complete consciousness*, I listened to those *quietly rejoicing colors.*

# CREDITS

# SOURCES

. . . . . . . . . . . . .

Nearly all the facts of Nabokov's life are taken from Brian Boyd's remarkable two-volume biography: *Vladimir Nabokov: The Russian Years*; *Vladimir Nabokov: The American Years*. The quotes are gleaned from novels and short stories (see the Comprehensive Quote Index); Nabokov's autobiography, *Speak, Memory*; his collection *Poems and Problems*; his essay *Nikolaï Gogol*; and his diaries. I have also used, on occasion, VN's *Strong Opinions*; his *Selected Letters*; his *Lectures on Literature*; *The Nabokov-Wilson Letters*; Dmitri Nabokov's "On Revisiting Father's Room"; and Stacy Schiff's *Véra (Mrs. Vladimir Nabokov)*. "The deductions," as Nabokov once wrote, "are my own."

# COMPREHENSIVE QUOTE INDEX

. . . . . . . . . . . . . . . . . . . . . . . . . . . . . . . . . . . . . . . . .

(NB: *Stories* refers to *The Stories of Vladimir Nabokov*. All VN quotes are from current Vintage editions. The *Selected Letters* and *Lectures on Literature* are from Harcourt Brace; the Brian Boyd biography from Princeton University Press; and Stacy Schiff's biography from Modern Library. All other publishers are cited in parentheses.)

## EPIGRAPH

"I trust the ravishing promises of the still breathing, still revolving verse, my face is wet with tears, my heart is bursting with happiness, and I know that this happiness is the greatest thing existing on earth." ( "Torpid Smoke," *Stories*, 400)

## FOREWORD

"If I had read as much as other men, I should be as ignorant." (*First We Read, Then We Write*, University of Iowa Press, 7)

"Dolly, an only child, born in Bras, married in 1840, at the tender and wayward age of fifteen, General Ivan Durmanov, Commander of Yukon Fortress and peaceful country gentleman, with lands in the Severn Tories (Severnïya Territorii), that tessellated protectorate still lovingly called 'Russian' Estoty, which commingles, granoblastically and organically, with 'Russian' Canady, otherwise 'French' Estoty, where not only French, but Macedonian and Bavarian settlers enjoy a halcyon climate under our Stars and Stripes." (*Ada*, 3)

"We are too civil to books. For a few golden sentences we will turn over and actually read a volume of 4 or 5 hundred pages." (*First We Read, Then We Write*, University of Iowa Press, 11)

"Noble iridescent creatures with translucent talons and mightily beating wings." (*Ada*, 20)

"Creative reader." (*Lectures on Literature*, 3)

"Crashing to our death from the top story of our birth and wondering with an immortal Alice in Wonderland at the patterns of the passing wall . . . These asides of the spirit, these footnotes in the volume of life are the highest form of consciousness." (*Lectures on Literature*, 373)

"The irrational, the illogical, the inexplicable." (*Lectures on Literature*, 377)

"The quotes it wore like claws." (*Ada*, 220)

"Perfect felicity." (*Bend Sinister*, 58)

"Beyond happiness." (*Lolita*, 166)


PROLOGUE

"I, Van Veen, salute you, life." (*Ada*, 567)


CHAPTER 1

"For the moon never beams, without bringing me dreams." (Edgar Allan Poe, "Annabel Lee," *Complete Stories and Poems,* Random House, 738)

"At 1 A.M. was raised from brief sleep by horrible anguish of the

'this-is-it' sort. *Discreetly* screamed, hoping to wake Véra in next
room yet failing to succeed (because I felt quite alright)." (Diary,
April 24, 1976; Boyd II, 656)

"Like Ovid's lyre." (*Selected Letters*, 552)

"Horrible shock." (Schiff, 356)

"Inspiration. Radiant insomnia. The flavour and snows of beloved
alpine slopes. A novel *without* an I, without a he, but with the narrator, the *gliding eye*, being implied throughout." (Diary, May 15,
1974; Boyd II, 644)

"A small dream audience in a walled garden. My audience consisted
of peacocks, pigeons, my long-dead parents, two cypresses, several young nurses crouching around, and a family doctor so old as
to be almost invisible." (*New York Times*, October 30, 1976; Boyd
II, 657)

"Only because you're not there. I would never mind a hospital stay if
I could take you, wrap you up in my top pocket and take you with
me." (Diary, September 21, 1976; Boyd II, 658)

"My literary regime is more fancy, but two hours of meditation,
between 2 A.M. and 4 A.M. when the effect of a first sleeping pill
evaporates and that of a second one has not begun, and a spell
of writing in the afternoon, are about all my new novel needs."
(Hugh A. Mulligan interview with VN, syndicated, *Hanover Star
Bulletin*, January 9, 1977; Boyd II, 658)

"I also intend to collect butterflies in Peru or in Iran before I pupate."
(Dieter Zimmer interview with VN, October 1966; Boyd II,
564)

"Everything begins anew." (Diary, March 19, 1977; Boyd II, 660)

"Mild delirium, temp. 37.5°. Is it possible that everything starts
anew?" (Diary, May 18, 1977; Boyd II, 660)

"Father still existed." ("On Revisiting Father's Room," Dmitri
Nabokov, *Vladimir Nabokov, A Tribute*, Morrow, 134)

"Now and then . . . one had an inkling of how deeply hurt he felt at the thought of being suddenly cut off from a life whose every detail gave him joy, and from a creative process in its fullest swing." ("On Revisiting Father's Room," Dmitri Nabokov, *Vladimir Nabokov, A Tribute*, Morrow, 136)

"A certain butterfly was already on the wing." ("On Revisiting Father's Room," Dmitri Nabokov, *Vladimir Nabokov, A Tribute*, Morrow, 136)

"Let's rent an airplane and crash." (Interviews with Dmitri Nabokov, February 1995–January 1997; Schiff, 360)

"There is another, very special box, containing a substantial part of the breathtakingly original *Original of Laura*, which would have been father's most brilliant novel, the most concentrated distillation of his creativity." ("On Revisiting Father's Room," Dmitri Nabokov, *Vladimir Nabokov, A Tribute*, Morrow, 129)

"They were something out of Shakespeare." (Azam Zanganeh interview with Dmitri Nabokov, September 2006)

"I do not know if it has ever been noted before that one of the main characteristics of life is discreteness." (*Pnin*, 20)

"Unless a film of flesh envelops us, we die. Man exists only insofar as he is separated from his surroundings." (*Pnin*, 20)

"The cranium is a space-traveler's helmet. Stay inside or you perish." (*Pnin*, 20)

"Death is divestment, death is communion." (*Pnin*, 20)

"It may be wonderful to mix with the landscape, but to do so is the end of the tender ego." (*Pnin*, 20)

"When a new item clicks into consciousness . . . my first mental reflex is the thought of bringing it to Father for approval, like a sea-levigated stone on a Riviera beach in childhood; and only a split-pang later do I realize there is no Father. Would he have liked my little offerings?" ("On Revisiting Father's Room," Dmitri Nabokov, *Vladimir Nabokov, A Tribute*, Morrow, 132)

"Margana"; "Tooth Transport." ("On Revisiting Father's Room," Dmitri Nabokov, *Vladimir Nabokov, A Tribute*, Morrow, 132)

CHAPTER 2

"The cradle rocks above an abyss, and common sense tells us that our existence is but a brief crack of light between two eternities of darkness." (*Speak, Memory*, 9)

"I felt myself plunged abruptly into a radiant and mobile medium that was none other than the pure element of time. One shared it—just as excited bathers share shining seawater—with creatures that were not oneself but that were joined to one by time's common flow." (*Speak, Memory*, 11)

"Indeed, from my present ridge of remote, isolated, almost uninhabited time, I see my diminutive self as celebrating, on that August day 1903, the birth of sentient life." (*Speak, Memory*, 11)

"Amidst the night of non-being." (George Feifer interview with VN, *Saturday Review*, November 27, 1976)

"Step, step, step . . ." (*Speak, Memory*, 60)

"Step, step, step and I would stumble, you would laugh." (VN to Elena Ivanovna Nabokov, October 16, 1920; Boyd I, 177)

"Curiously enough, one cannot read a book: one can only reread it." (*Lectures on Literature*, 3)

"Play!" (*Speak, Memory*, 41)

"A bright little gap in the park, five hundred yards away—or fifty years away from where I am now." (*Speak, Memory*, 41)

"Time, so boundless at first blush, was a prison." (*Speak, Memory*, 20)

"The prison of time is spherical and without exits." (*Speak, Memory*, 20)

"To love with all one's soul and leave the rest to fate." (*Speak, Memory*, 40)

" '*Vot zapomni* [now remember]' she would say in conspiratorial tones as she drew my attention to this or that loved thing in Vyra—a lark ascending the curds-and-whey sky of a dull spring day, heat lightning taking pictures of a distant line of trees in the night, the palette of maple leaves on brown sand, a small bird's cuneate footprints on new snow." (*Speak, Memory*, 40)

CHAPTER 3

"Lovely, sun-tanned, bad-tempered." (*Speak, Memory*, 149)

"The first to have the poignant power, by merely *not* letting her smile fade, of burning a hole in my sleep and jolting me into clammy consciousness, whenever I dreamed of her." (*Speak, Memory*, 210)

"Parted the fabric of fancy . . . tasted reality." (*Speak, Memory*, 232)

"That hushed July afternoon, when I discovered her standing quite still (only her eyes were moving) in a birch grove, she seemed to have been spontaneously generated there, among those watchful trees, with the silent completeness of a mythological manifestation." (*Speak, Memory*, 230)

"Always recall it as it looked first, fiercely braided into a thick plait that was looped up at the back of her head and tied there with a big bow of black silk." (*Speak, Memory*, 231)

"The following of such thematic designs through one's life should be, I think, the true purpose of autobiography." (*Speak, Memory*, 16)

"First and last things tend to have an adolescent note." (*Speak, Memory*, 1)

"Scepter of passion." (*Lolita*, 14)

"There it was, the same ominous flaw, the banal hollow note, and glib suggestion that our love was doomed since it could never recapture the miracle of its initial moments, the rustle and rush of those limes in the rain, the compassion of the wild countryside." (*Speak, Memory*, 238)

"The rapture of her identity." (*Ada*, 220)

"There might have been no Lolita at all had I not loved, one summer, a certain initial girl-child. In a princedom by the sea." (*Lolita*, 9)

"And then, without the least warning, a blue sea-wave swelled under my heart and, from a mat in a pool of sun, half-naked, kneeling, turning about on her knees, there was my Riviera love peering at me over dark glasses." (*Lolita*, 39)

"Dark-haired girl of eleven or twelve." (*Ada*, 37)

"She wore a white frock with a black jacket and there was a white bow in her long hair. He never saw that dress again and when he mentioned it in retrospective evocation she invariably retorted that he must have dreamt it, she never had one like that, never could have put on a dark blazer on such a hot day, but he stuck to his initial image of her to the last." (*Ada*, 37)

CHAPTER 4

"The only real thing in the world and the greatest mystery of all." (*Bend Sinister*, 188)

"How small the cosmos (a kangaroo's pouch would hold it), how paltry and puny in comparison to human consciousness, to a single individual recollection and its expression in words." (*Speak, Memory*, 24)

"A message scribbled in the dark." (*Pale Fire*, 41)

"That sudden window swinging open on a sunlit landscape." (George Feifer interview with VN, *Saturday Review*, November 27, 1976)

"A universe embraced by consciousness. The arms of consciousness reach out and grope, and the longer they are the better." (*Speak, Memory*, 218)

CHAPTER 5

"Entered an extravagant phase of sentiment and sensuality"; "a hundred different young men at once, all pursuing one changeful girl in a series of simultaneous or overlapping love affairs . . . , with very meager artistic results." (*Speak, Memory*, 240)

"Radiant truthfulness." (VN to Elena Sikorski; Schiff, 46)

"To the x degree." (*Ada*, 454)

"Frankly homosexual on the subject of translators." (VN to James
Laughlin; Boyd II, 45)

"The sharpest jealousy of all, is that between one woman and
another, and that between one littérateur and another. But when
a woman envies a littérateur, that can amount to $H_2SO_4$ [sulfuric
acid]." (VN to family; Schiff, 44)

"And her picture has often been reproduced by some mysterious
means of reflected color in the inner mirrors of my books."
(*Strong Opinions*, 191)

"Madame Nabokov is 38 Years Older than the Nymphet Lolita."
(Headline, *Paris Presse L'Intransigeant*, October 21, 1959)

"We are keeping this." (Interview with Keegan, November 14,
1997; Schiff, 167)

"I do get annoyed when people I never met impinge on my privacy
with false and vulgar assumptions—as for example Mr. Updike,
who in an otherwise clever article absurdly suggests that my fictional character, bitchy and lewd Ada, is, I quote, 'in a dimension
or two, Nabokov's wife.'" (James Mossman interview with VN,
BBC-2 *Review*, October 4, 1969; published in *The Listener*, October 23, 1969)

"What the hell, Sir, do you know about my married life?" (VN to
Hodgart, May 12, 1969; *Selected Letters*, 450–451)

"Posthaste, posthaste . . . The years are passing, my dear, and presently
nobody will know what you and I know." (*Speak, Memory*, 295)

"It has been suggested by doctors that we sometimes pooled our
minds when we dreamed." ("Scenes from the Life of a Double
Monster," *Stories*, 613)

"Precognitive flavor." (*Ada*, 361)

"Catch sight of the lining of time." (*Ada*, 227)

"You know, we are awfully like one another. In letters, for example:
We both love to (1) unobtrusively insert foreign words, (2) quote

from our favorite books, (3) translate our impressions from one sense (sense of sight, for example) into impressions of another sense (sense of taste, for example), (4) ask forgiveness at the end for some imaginary nonsense, and in many other ways." (VN to Véra Nabokov, January 8, 1924, Vladimir Nabokov Archive; Schiff, 38)

"Smelling of orchards in nymphetland." (*Lolita*, 92)

" 'Revolting,' 'super,' 'luscious,' 'goon.' " (*Lolita*, 65)

"Big handsome hunk of movieland manhood." (*Lolita*, 65)

"She would be thirteen on January 1. In two years or so she would cease being a nymphet and would turn into a 'young girl,' and then, into a 'college girl'—that horror of horrors." (*Lolita*, 65)

"We are not sex fiends! Emphatically, no killers are we. Poets never kill." (*Lolita*, 88)

"Madly in love." (*Lolita*, 19)

"A sparkling girleen . . . in a crimson frock, and this was in 1274, in Florence, at a private feast in the merry month of May." (*Lolita*, 19)

"A fair-haired nymphet of twelve running in the wind, in the pollen and dust, a flower in flight, in the beautiful plain as descried from the hills of Vaucluse." (*Lolita*, 19)

"Technically lovers." (*Lolita*, 132)

"Cruel and crafty"; "desperate, dying Humbert"; "despair and desperate meditation." (*Lolita*, 83)

"Wonderland"; "Humberland." (*Lolita*, 166)

"The corniest movies, the most cloying fudge." (*Lolita*, 166)

"Between a Hamburger and a Humburger, she would—invariably, with icy precision—plump for the former. There is nothing more atrociously cruel than an adored child." (*Lolita*, 166)

"Icebergs in paradise." (*Lolita*, 285)

"The remorse, the poignant sweetness of sobbing atonement, groveling love, the hopelessness of sensual reconciliation." (*Lolita*, 227)

"I loved you. I was a pentapod monster, but I loved you. I was despicable and brutal, and turpid, and everything, *mais je t'aimais, je t'aimais!* And there were times when I knew how you felt, and it was hell to know it, my little one. Lolita girl, brave Dolly Schiller." (*Lolita*, 284–285)

"Will Brown, Dolores, Colo."; "Harold Haze, Tombstone, Arizona"; "Ted Hunter, Cane, NH." (*Lolita*, 251)

"And there she was with her ruined looks and her adult, rope-veined narrow hands and her goose-flesh white arms, and her shallow ears, and her unkempt armpits, there she was (my Lolita!), hopelessly worn at seventeen . . . and I looked and looked at her, and knew as clearly as I know I am to die, that I loved her more than anything I had ever seen or imagined on earth, or hoped for anywhere else." (*Lolita*, 277)

"Lolita, light of my life, fire of my loins. My sin, my soul." (*Lolita*, 9)

"*Lolita* has no moral in tow." ("On a Book Entitled *Lolita*," *Lolita*, 314)

"Only insofar as it affords me what I shall bluntly call aesthetic bliss, that is a sense of being somehow, somewhere, connected with other states of being where art (curiosity, tenderness, kindness, ecstasy) is the norm." ("On a Book Entitled *Lolita*," *Lolita*, 314)

"The Russian way with two deep, dark 'a's." (*Ada*, 39)

"A void of light and a veil of shade that no force could overcome and pierce." (*Ada*, 103)

"Voluptuous, impermissible skin . . . her angular movements, her gazelle-grass odor, the sudden black stare of her wide-set eyes, and the rustic nudity under her dress." (*Ada*, 59)

"It would not be sufficient to say that in his love-making with Ada he discovered the pang, the *ogon'*, the agony of supreme 'reality.' Reality, better say, lost the quotes it wore like claws . . . For one spasm or two, he was safe. The new naked reality needed no tentacle or anchor; it lasted a moment, but could be repeated as often as he and she were physically able to make love." (*Ada*, 219–220)

"Orchards and orchidariums." (*Ada*, 409)

"Even eccentric police officers grew enamored with the glamour of incest." (*Ada*, 409)

"In both sisters, the front teeth were a trifle too large and the nether lip too fat for the ideal beauty of marble death; and because their noses were permanently stuffed, both girls (especially later, at fifteen and twelve) looked a little dreamy and dazed in profile." (*Ada*, 104)

"Darkly flossed." (*Ada*, 59)

"Showed a slight stipple of bright floss and her chub was dusted with copper." (*Ada*, 144)

"A macédoine of intuition, stupidity, naïveté and cunning." (*Ada*, 152)

"The irresistible rake." (*Ada*, 588)

"We are watched by Lucette, whom I shall strangle some day." (*Ada*, 148)

"Absolutely sterile despite his prowesses." (*Ada*, 394)

"Pure joyousness and Arcadian innocence." (*Ada*, 588)

"Half *poule*, half *puella*" (*Ada*, 372)

"I adore (*obozhayu*), I adore, I adore, I adore more than life you, you (*tebya, tebya*), I ache for you unbearably ( *ya toskuyu po tebe nevinosimo*)." (*Ada*, 411)

"Apricot-bloomed forearm." (*Ada*, 411)

"Bird of paradise." (*Ada*, 387)

"I want Van, and not intangible admiration—" "Intangible? You goose. You may gauge it, you may brush it once very lightly, with the knuckles of your gloved hand. I said knuckles. I said once. That will do. I can't kiss you. Not even your burning face. Goodbye, pet." (*Ada*, 387)

"The fire of Lucette's amber runs through the night of Ada's odor and ardor, and stops at the threshold of Van's lavender goat. Ten, eager, evil, loving, long fingers, belonging to two different young demons caress their helpless bed pet." (*Ada*, 419–420)

"*Tonen'kiy-tonen'kiy* (thin little) layer." (*Ada*, 464)

"At every slap and splash of cold white salt, she heaved with anise-flavored nausea and there was an increasing number, okay, numbness, in her neck and arms. As she began losing track of herself, she thought it proper to inform a series of receding Lucettes—telling them to pass it on and on in a trick-crystal regression—that what death amounted to was only a more complete assortment of the infinite fractions of solitude." (*Ada*, 494)

"All in all, I suppose I have had her about a thousand times. She is my whole life." (*Ada*, 440)

"The highest ridge of their twenty-one-year-old love: its complicated, dangerous, ineffably radiant coming of age." (*Ada*, 521)

"Oh, Van, oh Van, we did not love her enough. *That's* whom you should have married, the one sitting feet up, in ballerina black, on the stone balustrade, and then everything would have been alright—I would have stayed with you both in Ardis Hall, and instead of that happiness, handed out gratis, instead of all that we *teased* her to death!" (*Ada*, 586)

"Glittering 'now.' " (*Ada*, 556)

"Into the finished book, into Eden or Hades, into the prose of the book or the poetry of its blurb." (*Ada*, 587)

CHAPTER 6

"What were the three great losses of Na-BOAK-off?" (Azam Zanganeh interview with Dmitri Nabokov, September 2006)

"An island of happiness in the clear north of my being." ("Spring in Fialta," *Stories*, 414)

"Tamara, Russia, the wildwood grading into old gardens . . . the sight of my mother getting down on her hands and knees to kiss

and never saw again. One may thus imagine a retired business man in the Boston of 1875, casually telling his wife of having dreamt the other night that together with a young Russian or Pole whom he had once met in Germany when he was young himself he was buying a clock and a cloak in a shop of antiques." (*Gogol*, New Directions, 26)

"Syncopal kick . . . would not have missed for worlds." (*Speak, Memory*, 250)

"Homesickness has been with me a sensuous and particular matter." (*Speak, Memory*, 250)

"Karakuls of the dark Tauric pines . . . positively Baghdadian." (*Speak, Memory*, 244)

"I am infinitely happy, and so agitated and sad today." (VN to EIN, April 26, 1920, VNA; Boyd I, 175)

"There was always that initial pang one feels just before time, caught unawares, again dons its familiar mask." (*Speak, Memory*, 49)

"Thus, in a way, I inherited an exquisite simulacrum—the beauty of intangible property, unreal estate—and this proved a splendid training for the endurance of later losses." (*Speak, Memory*, 40)

"What it would be to actually see again my former surroundings, I can hardly imagine." (*Speak, Memory*, 250)


CHAPTER 7

"The mirror brims with brightness; a bumblebee has entered the room and bumps against the ceiling. Everything is as it should be, nothing will ever change, nobody will ever die." (*Speak, Memory*, 77)

"The incalculable amount of tenderness contained in the world . . . the fate of this tenderness, which is either crushed, or wasted, or transformed into madness." ( "Signs and Symbols," *Stories*, 601)

"The first creatures on earth to become aware of time were also the first creatures to smile." (*Speak, Memory*, 22)

"*Zaychik*"; "sun blick." (*Ada*, 286)

"We can know the time, we can know a time. We can never know Time." (*Ada*, 563)

"Our senses are simply not meant to perceive it. It is like——" (*Ada*, 563)

"We feel it as moving only because it is the medium where growth and change take place or where things stop, like stations." (Yearbook, 1951, VNA; Boyd II, 379)

"Eighty years quickly passed—a matter of changing a slide in a magic lantern." (*Ada*, 585)

"But *this* . . . is certain, this is reality, this is pure fact—this forest, this moss, your hand, the ladybird on my leg, this cannot be taken away, can it? (it will, it was). *This* has all come together *here*, no matter how the paths twisted, and fooled each other, and got fouled up, they inevitably met here!" (*Ada*, 124)

"We can never enjoy the *true* Present, which is an instant of zero duration." (*Ada*, 550)

"Flowering of the Present." (*Ada*, 549)

"The hush of pure memory." (*Speak, Memory*, 309)

"Hammock and honey: eighty years later he could still recall with the young pang of the original joy his falling in love with Ada." (*Ada*, 59)

"Memory met imagination halfway in the hammock of his boyhood's dawns. At ninety-four he liked retracing that first amorous summer not as a dream he had just had but as a recapitulation of consciousness to sustain him in the small gray hours between shallow sleep and the first pill of the day." (*Ada*, 59)

"In 1884, during my first summer at Ardis, I seduced your daughter, who was then twelve. Our torrid affair lasted till my return to Riverlane; it was resumed last June, four years later. That happiness has been the greatest event in my life, and I have no regrets." (*Ada*, 244)

"I confess I do not believe in time." (*Speak, Memory*, 9)

"Glittering 'now.' " (*Ada*, 556)

"The singular little thrill of following dark byways in strange towns, knowing well that he would discover nothing, save filth, and ennui, and discarded 'merry-cans' with 'Billy' labels, and the jungle jingles of exported jazz coming from syphilitic cafés. He often felt that the famed cities, the museums, the ancient torture house and the suspended garden were but places on the map of his own madness." (*Ada*, 449–450)

"Pure Time, Perceptual Time, Tangible Time, free of content, context and running commentary." (*Ada*, 539)

CHAPTER 8

"Tip, leaf, dip, relief—the instant it all took to happen seemed to me not so much a fraction of time as a fissure in it, a missed heartbeat." (*Speak, Memory*, 217)

"Applying his fiery sarcasm." (*Speak, Memory*, 238)

"Would never, never be a writer." (*Speak, Memory*, 238)

"Dying nightly, I am glad / to rise again at the appointed hour. / The next day is a dewdrop of paradise / and the day past, a diamond." (VN to EIN, November 25, 1921; Boyd I, 188)

"This little poem will prove to you that my mood is as radiant as ever. If I live to be a hundred, my soul will still go round in short trousers." (VN to EIN, November 25, 1921; Boyd I, 187)

"The centuries will roll by, and schoolboys will yawn over the history of our upheavals; everything will pass, but my happiness, dear, my happiness will remain, in the moist reflection of a streetlamp, in the cautious bend of stone steps that descend into the canal's black waters, in the smiles of a dancing couple, in everything with which God so generously surrounds human loneliness." ("A Letter That Never Reached Russia," *Stories*, 140)

"A practical handbook: *How to Be Happy*." (*The Gift*, 328)

"Baffling mirror." ("On a Book Entitled *Lolita*," *Lolita*, 316–317)

"The monster of grim commonsense that is lumbering up the steps to whine that the book is not for the general public, that the book will never never—And right then, just before it blurts out the word *s, e, double-l,* false commonsense must be shot dead." (*Lectures on Literature*, 380)

"Topical trash." ("On a Book Entitled *Lolita*," *Lolita*, 316–317)

"All 'general ideas' (so easily acquired, so profitably resold) must necessarily remain but worn passports allowing their bearer short cuts from one area of ignorance to another." (*Eugene Onegin*, 1:8; Boyd II, 340)

"What the artist perceives is, primarily, the *difference* between things." (*Despair*, 41)

"Not in words but in shadows of words." (*Strong Opinions*, 30)

"It was not the sly demon smile of remembered or promised ardor, but the exquisite human glow of happiness and helplessness." (*Ada*, 286)

"Bamboo bridge." (*Strong Opinions*, 169)

"Sees everything that happens in one point of space." (*Speak, Memory*, 218)

"Feels everything that happens in one point of time." (*Speak, Memory*, 218)

"A car (New York license plate) passes along the road, a child bangs the screen door of a neighboring porch, an old man yawns in a misty Turkestan orchard, a granule of cinder-gray sand is rolled by the wind on Venus, a Docteur Jacques Hirsch in Grenoble puts on his reading glasses, and trillions of other such trifles occur— all forming an instantaneous and transparent organism of events, of which the poet (sitting in a lawn chair, at Ithaca, N.Y.) is the nucleus." (*Speak, Memory*, 218)

"Only in the sense that they are true creatures." (*Gogol*, New Directions, 41)

"Splendid insincerity." (*Poems and Problems*, McGraw-Hill, 15)

"Zoo of words." (*Speak, Memory*, 233)

"Wings and claws." (*Lolita*, 312)

"Fellow who sends planets spinning." (*Lectures on Literature*, 2)

"Says 'go!' allowing the world to flicker and to fuse." (*Lectures on Literature*, 2)

"Those berries are edible. That speckled creature that bolted across my path might be tamed. That lake between those trees will be called Lake Opal or, more artistically, Dishwater Lake. That mist is a mountain—and that mountain must be conquered." (*Lectures on Literature*, 2)

"Unique surprises." (*Lectures on Literature*, 2)

"Fancy is fertile only when it is futile." (*Gogol*, New Directions, 76)

"Nabokov writes prose the only way it should be written, that is, ecstatically." (John Updike, *New Yorker*, September 26, 1964)

"Green rainy day." (*Ada*, 26)

"Blue snow of notepaper." (*Ada*, 332)

"Opalescent knee." (*Lolita*, 12)

"Crystal sleep." (*Lolita*, 123)

"Old Demon, iridescent wings humped, half-rose but sank back again." (*Ada*, 245)

"Jurors! If my happiness could have talked, it would have filled that genteel hotel with a deafening roar." (*Lolita*, 123)

"Failing and fadings"; "the fatigue of its fugue—the last resort of nature, felicitous alliterations (when flowers and flies mime one another), the coming of a first pause in late August, a first silence in early September." (*Ada*, 139)

"A state of acute indigestion." (*Ada*, 355)

"After letting winds go free." (*Ada*, 140)

"A steady hum of happiness." (*Ada*, 574)

"All of this might sound nice in another language." (*New York Times*, January 11, 1942)

"Sinuosity, which is my own and which only at first glance may seem awkward or obscure. Why not have the reader re-read a sentence now and then? It won't hurt him." (*Selected Letters*, 77)

"There was nobody called 'Joan of Arc.' I prefer, however, her real name, Joaneta Darc. It would be rather silly, for instance, if in a *New Yorker* issue of 2500, I were alluded to as 'Voldemar of Cornell' or 'Nabo of Leningrad.' So, on the whole, I would like to retain 'fatidic accents' and 'Joaneta Darc' if possible." (VN to Katherine White, March 4, 1949, VNA; Boyd II, 137)

"What I loved best was the broken English." (VN to VéN, October 7, 1942; Boyd II, 51)

"Some of your phrases are so good they almost give me an erection—and at my age it is not easy, you know." (Morris Bishop, Yearbook, 1951, VNA; Boyd II, 192)

"That marvelous lectern at which he would begin his writing day is gone. But here, propped against the desk's rear parapet, is the unframed, faded, and dusty reproduction of Fra Beato Angelico's *L'Annunciazione*, brought from Italy by Aunt Elena, with the rigid angel making his announcement on one knee." ("On Revisiting Father's Room," Dmitri Nabokov, *Vladimir Nabokov, A Tribute*, Morrow, 127)

"All colors made me happy: even gray." (*Pale Fire*, 34)

"Long, black, blue-ocellated." (*Ada*, 180)

"Permanent broad smile." (Eds. Alfred Appel, Jr., Charles Newman, *Nabokov: criticism, reminiscences, translations, and tributes*, Northwestern University Press, 124)

"I trust you will plunge into the book as into a blue ice hole, gasp, re-plunge, and then (around p. 126) emerge and sleigh home, metaphorically, feeling the tingling and delightful warmth reach you on the way from my strategically placed bonfires." (VN to Minton, December 6, 1961, VNA; Boyd II, 424)

CHAPTER 9

"Record of my love affair." ("On a Book Entitled *Lolita*," *Lolita*, 316)

"Caress the details! The divine details!" (*Lectures on Literature*, xxiii)

"The lyrical, epic, tragic, but never Arcadian American wilds. They are beautiful, heartrendingly beautiful . . . Venus came and went." (*Lolita*, 168)

"One afternoon they were climbing the glossy-limbed shattal tree . . . 'I was seeking some kind of support.' " (*Ada*, 94–95)

CHAPTER 10

"A Poet was I, and I sang that . . ." (Dante, *Inferno*, George Routledge and Sons, 4)

"American inhabitants." (*Speak, Memory*, 186)

"As American as April in Arizona." (*Strong Opinions*, 98)

"Infinitely docile Russian tongue." ("On a Book Entitled *Lolita*," *Lolita*, 316–317)

CHAPTER 11

"When I was younger, I ate some butterflies in Vermont to see if they were poisonous. I didn't see any difference between a Monarch butterfly and a Viceroy. The taste of both was vile, but I had no ill effects. They tasted like almonds and perhaps a green cheese combination. I ate them raw. I held one in one hot little hand and one in the other. Will you eat some with me tomorrow for breakfast?" (Robert Boyle interview with VN, *Sports Illustrated*, 1959; Boyd II, 383–384)

"Summer *soomerki*—the lovely Russian word for dusk. Time: a dim point in the first decade of this unpopular century. Place: latitude 59° north from your equator, longitude 100° east from my writing hand." (*Speak, Memory*, 81)

"As a pretty boy in knickerbockers and sailor cap; as a lanky cosmopolitan expatriate in flannel bags and beret; as a fat hatless old man in shorts." (*Speak, Memory*, 125)

"How many jeers, how many conjectures and questions have I had occasion to hear when, overcoming my embarrassment, I walked through the village with my net! 'Well that's nothing,' said my father, 'you should have seen the faces of the Chinese when I was collecting once on some holy mountain, or the look the progressive schoolmistress in a Volga town gave me when I explained to her what I was doing in that ravine.' " (*The Gift*, 108–109)

"The highest enjoyment of timelessness—in a landscape selected at random—is when I stand among rare butterflies and their food plants. This is ecstasy, and behind the ecstasy is something else, which is hard to explain. It is like a momentary vacuum into which rushes all that I love. A sense of oneness with sun and stone. A thrill of gratitude to whom it may concern—to the contrapuntal genius of human fate or to tender ghosts humoring a lucky mortal." (*Speak, Memory*, 139)

"Swimming, sloping, elusive something . . . which seemed still to retain the shadows it had absorbed of ancient, fabulous forests where there were more birds than tigers and more fruit than thorns, and where, in some dappled depth, man's mind had been born." (*Speak, Memory*, 298)

"Without whom the policemen couldn't distinguish a butterfly from an angel or from a bat." (Bernard Pivot television interview with VN, *Apostrophes*, 1975)

"Some gaudy moth or butterfly." (*Lolita*, 110)

"Creeping white flies." (*Lolita*, 156)

"That bug patiently walking up the inside of that window." (*Lolita*, 211)

"Professor Nabonidus"; "accursed insect." (*Ada*, 158)

"I discovered in nature the nonutilitarian delights that I sought in art. Both were a form of magic, both were a game of intricate enchantment and deception." (*Speak, Memory*, 125)

"When one realizes that for all its blunders and boners the inner texture of life is also a matter of inspiration and precision." (*Lectures on Literature*, 381)

"The enormous moth which in a state of repose assumes the image of a snake looking at you; of a tropical geometrid colored in perfect imitation of a species of butterfly infinitely removed from it in nature's system." (*The Gift*, 110–111)

"A bird comes and wonders for a second. Is it two bugs? Where is the head? Which side is which? In that split second the butterfly is gone. That second saves that individual and that species." "It has a curiously formed letter C. It mimics a chink of light through a dead leaf. Isn't that wonderful? Isn't that humorous?" (Robert Boyle for *Sports Illustrated*, 1959; Boyd II, 383–384)

"Tender, ravishing, almost human happiness." ("Christmas," *Stories*, 136)

"Most probably he visited Granada and Murcia and Albarracin, and then traveled farther still, to Surinam or Taprobane; and one can hardly doubt that he saw all the glorious bugs he had longed to see—" ("The Aurelian," *Stories*, 258)

"Experienced still keener pangs when he did, for never would he catch the loftily flapping Brazilian morphos, so ample and radiant that they cast an azure reflection upon one's hand, never come upon those crowds of African butterflies closely stuck like innumerable fancy flags into the rich black mud and rising in a colored cloud when his shadow approached." ("The Aurelian," *Stories*, 254)

"The song of a Tuscan Firecrest or a Sitka Kinglet in a cemetery cypress; a minty whiff of Summer Savory or Yerba Buena on a coastal slope; the dancing flitter of a Holly Blue or an Echo Azure." (*Ada*, 71)

"All was beautiful as neither nature nor art can contrive, beautiful as it only is when these two come together." (*Gogol*, New Directions, 88)

"He told me about the odors of butterflies—musk and vanilla; about the voices of butterflies; about the piercing sound given out by the monstrous caterpillar of a Malayan hawkmoth . . . about the cunning butterfly in the Brazilian forest which imitates the whir of a local bird. He told me about the incredible artistic wit of mimetic disguise." (*The Gift*, 110)

"Myriads of white Pierids . . . floating further, to settle on trees toward nighttime which stand until morning as if bestrewn with snow—and then taking off again to continue their journey— whither? Why? A tale not yet finished by nature or else forgotten . . . With a strange crazy flight unlike anything else, the bleached, hardly recognizable butterfly, choosing a dry glade, 'wheels' in and out of the Leshino firs, and by the end of the summer, on thistleheads, on asters, its lovely pink-flushed offspring is already reveling in life. 'Most moving of all,' added my father, 'is that on the first cold days a reverse phenomenon is observed, the ebb: the butterfly hastens southward, for the winter, but of course it perishes before it reaches the warmth.' " (*The Gift*, 111)

## CHAPTER 12

"Give me the creative reader; this is a tale for him." (*Gogol*, New Directions, 140)

"Emperors, dictators, priests, puritans, philistines, political moralists, policemen, postmasters, and prigs." (*Lectures on Russian Literature*, 10)

"Curiosity is insubordination in its purest form." (*Bend Sinister*, 40)

"Ever drifting down the stream—

Lingering in the golden gleam—

Life, what is it but a dream?"

(Lewis Carroll, *Through the Looking-Glass*, Random House, 240)

"Unknown dreamers." (*Ada*, 122)

"Ardis Hall—the Ardors and Arbors of Ardis—this is the leitmotiv rippling through *Ada*, an ample and delightful chronicle, whose

principal part is staged in a dream-bright America—for are not
our childhood memories comparable to Vineland-borne caravelles,
indolently encircled by the white birds of dream?" (*Ada*, 588)
"The rest of Van's story turns frankly and colorfully upon his long
love-affair with Ada. It is interrupted by her marriage to an Arizonian cattle-breeder whose fabulous ancestor discovered our country. After her husband's death our lovers are reunited." (*Ada*, 588)
"Before we can pause to take breath and quietly survey the new surroundings into which the writer's magic carpet has, as it were,
spilled us." (*Ada*, 588)

## CHAPTER 13

"The crunch of happiness." (John Updike, *New Yorker*, February 26,
1972)
"Fabulous, insane, exertions that left me limp and azure-barred."
(*Lolita*, 285)
"I realized that the world does not represent a struggle at all, or
a predaceous sequence of chance events, but shimmering bliss,
beneficent trepidation, a gift bestowed on us and unappreciated."
("Beneficence," *Stories*, 77)
"For a while he lay on the black divan, but that seemed only to
increase the pressure of passionate obsession. He decided to
return to the upper floor by the cochlea." (*Ada*, 209)
"When I first met Tamara—to give her a name concolorous with
her real one—she was fifteen, and I was a year older. The place
was the rugged but comely country (black fir, white birch, peatbogs, hayfields, and barrens) just south of St. Petersburg." (*Speak,
Memory*, 229)
"The town was newly built, or rebuilt, on the flat floor of a seven-
thousand-foot-high valley; it would soon bore Lo, I hoped, and
we would spin on to California, to the Mexican border, to mythical bays, saguaro deserts, fata morganas." (*Lolita*, 239)

"And the savor of the grass stalk I was chewing mingled with the cuckoo's note and the fritillary's take-off." (*Speak, Memory*, 219)

"A large, alabaster-based kerosene lamp is steered into the gloaming. Gently it floats and comes down; the hand of memory, now in a footman's white glove, places it in the center of a round table." (*Speak, Memory*, 100)

"A very light cloud was opening its arms and moving toward a slightly more substantial one belonging to another, more sluggish, heavenlogged system." (*Lolita*, 307)

"Consider the tricks of an acrobatic caterpillar (of the Lobster Moth) which in infancy looks like bird's dung, but after molting develops scrabbly hymenopteroid appendages and baroque characteristics, allowing the extraordinary fellow to play two parts at once." (*Speak, Memory*, 124)

"It was also a particularly severe winter, producing as much snow as Mademoiselle might have expected to find in the hyperborean gloom of remote Muscovy." (*Speak, Memory*, 97)

"The word for rainbow, a primary, but decidedly muddy, rainbow, is in my private language the hardly pronounceable: *kzspygv*." (*Speak, Memory*, 35)

"I had nothing—except one token light in the potentially refulgent chandelier of Mademoiselle's bedroom, whose door, by our family doctor's decree (I salute you, Dr Sokolov!), remained slightly ajar. Its vertical line of lambency (which a child's tears could transform into dazzling rays of compassion) was something I could cling to, since in absolute darkness my head would swim and my mind melt in a travesty of the death struggle." (*Speak, Memory*, 109)

"As I focused my eyes upon a kidney-shaped flower bed (and noted one pink petal lying on the loam and a small ant investigating its decayed edge) or considered the tanned midriff of a birch trunk where some hoodlum had stripped it of its papery, pepper-and-salt bark, I really believed . . ." (*Speak, Memory*, 221)

"My Lolita . . . smelling of orchards in nymphetland; awkward and fey, and dimly depraved, the lower buttons of her shirt unfastened." (*Lolita*, 92)

"The colored spot, the stab of an afterimage, with which the lamp one had just turned off wounds the palpebral night." (*Speak, Memory*, 34)

"Demon's senses must have been influenced by a queer sort of incestuous (whatever the term means) pleasure . . . when he fondled, and savored, and delicately parted and defiled, in unmentionable but fascinating ways, flesh (*une chair*) that was both that of his wife and that of his mistress, the blended and brightened charms of twin peris, an Aquamarina both single and double, an orgy of epithelial alliteration." (*Ada*, 19)

"When that pearly language of hers purled and scintillated." (*Speak, Memory*, 113)

"Today I have at last perfectly matched *v* with 'Rose Quartz' in Maerz and Paul's *Dictionary of Color*." (*Speak, Memory*, 35)

"Its tremendous desk with nothing upon its waste of dark leather but a huge curved paper knife, a veritable scimitar of yellow ivory carved from a mammoth's tusk." (*Speak, Memory*, 72)

"The interest that perfect strangers showed in regard to him seemed alive with dark stratagems and incalculable dangers (beautiful word, stratagem—a treasure in a cave)." (*Gogol*, New Directions, 59)

"He had beautiful manners, a sweet temper, an unforgettable handwriting, all thorns and bristles (the like of which I have seen only in the letters from madmen, that, alas, I sometimes receive since the year of grace 1958), and an unlimited fund of obscene stories (which he fed me sub rosa in a dreamy, velvety voice, without using one gross expression)." (*Speak, Memory*, 168–169)

"The Swallowtail of June 1906 was still in the larval stage on a road-side umbellifer." (*Speak, Memory*, 122)

"Hysterical little nymphs might, I knew, run up all kinds of temperature—even exceeding a fatal count. And I would have given her a sip of hot spiced wine, and two aspirins, and kissed the fever away, if, upon an examination of her lovely uvula, one of the gems of her body, I had not seen that it was a burning red." (*Lolita*, 240)

CHAPTER 14

"A pessimist and, like all pessimists, a ridiculously unobservant man." ("An Affair of Honor," *Stories*, 218)

"The very essence of things." (Martha Updike, *Libération*, August 31, 1986; Boyd II, 173)

"I know more than I can express in words, and the little I can express would not have been expressed, had I not known more." (*Strong Opinions*, 65)

"Lunatic who constantly felt that all the parts of a landscape and movements of inanimate objects were a complex code of allusion to his own being, so that the whole universe seemed to be conversing about him by means of signs." (*Gogol*, New Directions, 59)

"Some law of logic should fix the number of coincidences, in a given domain, after which they cease to be coincidences, and form, instead, the living organism of a new truth." (*Ada*, 361)

"Those dazzling coincidences that logicians loathe and poets love." (*Lolita*, 31)

"Not text, but texture." (*Pale Fire*, 44)

"Not flimsy nonsense, but a web of sense. / Yes! It sufficed that I in life could find / Some kind of link-and-bobolink, some kind / Of correlated pattern in the game." (*Pale Fire*, 44)

"Try, Bunny, it is the noblest sport in the world." (*Dear Bunny, Dear*

*Volodya: The Nabokov-Wilson Letters, 1940–1971,* University of California Press, 76)

"Oneness with sun and stone." (*Speak, Memory,* 139)

"Dream Blue." (*Lolita,* 227)

"Hi, Melmoth, thanks a lot, old fellow." (*Lolita,* 307)

"Sealyham cedar." (*Ada,* 211)

"Fox-furred segments." (*Ada,* 449)

"One of those repetitions, one of those thematic 'voices' with which, according to all the rules of harmony, destiny enriches the life of observant men." (*The Gift,* 199)

"Thrill and glamour"; "finds in the most ordinary pleasures as well as in the seemingly meaningless adventures." (*Glory,* ii–iii)

"Liquid verbs in *ahla* and in *ili.*" ("An Evening of Russian Poetry," *New Yorker,* March 3, 1945)

"An unequivocal, and indeed all-deciding, sign of continued being behind the veil of time, beyond the flesh of space." (*Ada,* 452)

"We are not going anywhere, we are sitting at home. The other world surrounds us always and is not at all the end of some pilgrimage. In our earthly house, windows are replaced by mirrors; the door, until a given time, is closed; but air comes in through the cracks." (*The Gift,* 310)

"Glassy darkness"; "the strangeness of life, the strangeness of its magic, as if a corner of it had been turned back for an instant"; "its unusual lining." (*The Gift,* 183)

"All this skein of random thoughts, like everything else as well—the seams and sleaziness of the spring day, the ruffle of the air, the coarse, variously intercrossing threads of confused sounds—was but the reverse side of a magnificent fabric." (*The Gift,* 314)

" 'Iceling' or 'inglice.' I think that *some day* that will happen to the whole of life." (*The Gift,* 349)

"Galaxies divine." (*Pale Fire,* 69)

"Certainly not then—not in dreams—but when one is wide awake, at moments of robust joy and achievement, on the highest terrace of consciousness, that mortality has a chance to peer beyond its own limits, from the mast, from the past and its castle-tower. And although nothing much can be seen through the mist, there is somehow the blissful feeling that one is looking in the right direction." (*Speak, Memory*, 50)

## CHAPTER 15

"Sun-spangled." (*Speak, Memory*, 30)

"Mesh of sunshine." (*Speak, Memory*, 33)

"Icicles . . . gloriously burned in the low sun." (*Speak, Memory*, 103)

"Sun broke into geometrical gems." (*Speak, Memory*, 105)

"Sea of sunshot greenery." (*Speak, Memory*, 136)

"Lucid, turquoise space." (*Speak, Memory*, 213)

"Brilliant convulsions." (*Speak, Memory*, 213)

"Unusual euphoria of lightness." (*Speak, Memory*, 37)

"Sun-mottled." (*Speak, Memory*, 80)

"Red sun of desire and decision." (*Lolita*, 71)

"Roundlets of live light." (*Ada*, 51)

"Brilliant veil." (*Speak, Memory*, 231)

"Apple-green light." (*Lolita*, 41)

"Lurid gleam." (*Speak, Memory*, 44)

"Dusk-mellowed." (*Lolita*, 146)

"Sealskin-lined scarlet skies." (*Pale Fire*, 85)

"Beaming vestige of sunlight." (*Ada*, 154)

"Handful of fabulous lights." (*Speak, Memory*, 24)

"Under the pale star-dusted firmament." (*Ada*, 116)

"Radiant night, satiated with moonlight"; "iridescent Persian poem." (*Ada*, 413)

"Moth-flaked porchlight." (*Ada*, 262)

"Golden ghouls or the passing fancies of the garden." (*Ada*, 72)

"Arabesques of lighted windows." (*Lolita*, 14)

"Trick of harlequin light." (*Lolita*, 263)

"Magical lumps of calcium carbide." (*Speak, Memory*, 233)

"Selenian glow." (*Lolita*, 293)

"Light collapses." (*Speak, Memory*, 110)

"Sudden radiance of a lone lamp." (*Speak, Memory*, 99)

"Emerald lantern." (*Ada*, 211)

"Arena of radiance." (*Speak, Memory*, 134)

"Translucent green tone of grapes." (*Speak, Memory*, 119)

"Bright leer of madness." (*Ada*, 154)

"Pallor shone"; "blackness blazed." (*Ada*, 58)

"Scaly light." (*Ada*, 116)

"Tender, moist gleam." (*Speak, Memory*, 231)

"Double gleam." (*Speak, Memory*, 50)

"Limpid and luminous letter." (*Strong Opinions*, 25)

"Prismatic Babel." (Orhan Pamuk, *Other Colors*, Knopf, 155)

"Lebanese blue." (*Ada*, 204)

"Layers of light." (*Lolita*, 42)

"Emerald lantern." (*Ada*, 211)

"Violet-tinged nimbus of gaslight." (*Speak, Memory*, 90)

"Small luminous beetle." (*Ada*, 71)

"Limpid dawn." (*Speak, Memory*, 295)

"Dappled sun." (*Lolita*, 41)

"Pale-lemon light"; "glades of lucid smoothness." (*Ada*, 555)

"Sparkled from end to end." ("Perfection," *Stories*, 343)

"Gleam of complete consciousness." (*Speak, Memory*, 22)

"Quietly rejoicing colors." (*Lolita*, 36)

# PHOTOGRAPHY INDEX

CHAPTER 5

12 + 38. (Poolside of Montreux Palace, Switzerland, Summer 1966, Philippe Halsman, © Philippe Halsman / Magnum)

He and You. (Montreux Palace, Switzerland, October 1968, Philippe Halsman, © Philippe Halsman / Magnum)

CHAPTER 6

Rural laborer. (Estate of Domaine Beaulieu, France, Spring or Summer 1923, © Dmitri Nabokov)

Émigré passport, April 1940. (Paris, France, April 1940, © Dmitri Nabokov)

CHAPTER 10

VN and me by Lake Como. (Ithaca, New York, late 1957, © The Department of Manuscripts and University Archives, Cornell University Library; montage by Lila Azam Zanganeh)

Dmitri, conquering his own America. (Junction of East Ridge and North Face near the summit of Grand Teton, Jackson Hole, Wyoming, July 1952, © Dmitri Nabokov)

CHAPTER 11

"My soul will still go round in short trousers." (Zermatt, Switzerland, 1962, Horst Tappe, © Horst Tappe Foundation)

CHAPTER 14

Wide awake. (Montreux, Switzerland, September 1966, Philippe Halsman, © Philippe Halsman / Magnum)

## ACKNOWLEDGMENTS

I would like to thank Dmitri Nabokov for his immense kindness and tremendous support, my editors Alane Salierno Mason and Alexis Kirschbaum for their uniquely meticulous and passionate work, as well as Olivier Cohen, who so graciously led the way. My deep gratitude also goes to Bijan Saffari, for telling me about the meaning of the butterfly which sat on his shoulder in Montreux; Françoise Grellet, for teaching me the particulars of the English language; Judith Crist, for first inspiring me to write; Andreas Guest, for grasping all the happiness of *Ada*; and Jakuta Alikavazovic, for turning up one afternoon as my Nabokovian sibling. I shall always be grateful for the extraordinary feedback, at various times, of Brian Boyd, Larissa MacFarquhar, Tommy Karshan, Nina Khrushcheva, Jim Hanks, Jesse Lichtenstein, Leah Pisar, Topaz Page-Green, Pierre Demarty, Rava Azeredo da Silveira, Jean-Louis Jeannelle,

Marie-Laure Geoffray, Julie Peghini, and Justine Landau. Their generosity went beyond anything I might ever have imagined or hoped for.

## ABOUT THE AUTHOR

. . . . . . . . . . . . . . . . . . . . . . . . . . .

LILA AZAM ZANGANEH was born in Paris. Twenty years later, she moved to the United States. *The Enchanter* is her first book.